Diamond in the Emerald City

The Story of SAFECO Field

THE SEATTLE MARINERS
SEATTLE, WASHINGTON

JOHN W. ELLIS   NATALIE FOBES   FRANK WETZEL

A Diamond in the Emerald City

John W. Ellis, Natalie Fobes, Frank Wetzel

Includes index.

Library of Congress Card Number: 99-071044

ISBN: 0-9670454-0-1

Printed in Hong Kong

ACKNOWLEDGEMENTS

The idea for a book to commemorate the opening of SAFECO Field is as old as the idea for a new ballpark. However, we got serious about the subject in the spring of 1997 as everyone waited for construction to begin. When all hurdles were cleared and work started in June, the book project began as well. On the job from the beginning were Bob Hartley, longtime communications consultant to the Mariners, and his firm, the Rockey Company. We arranged with Hartley to manage the book project from beginning to end. Also on hand at the outset was Natalie Fobes, a Seattle-based professional photographer whom the Mariners contracted with for the duration of work on the ballpark. Her task was to capture the creation of a ballpark in photographic images. We hope you agree that she did a remarkable job.

This is our way of saying that the book is no weekend wonder.

The publications team, including Mariners officials, has worked on this production for two years.

The time and effort are two of the main reasons why the Mariners are especially proud of this book as a chronicle of the work required to bring you SAFECO Field. Our objective was to present a book that contains one-of-a-kind photographs, unmatched for access and quality. Furthermore, we wanted text that caught the flavor and history of baseball in the Pacific Northwest, and especially Seattle.

As an accompaniment to Ms. Fobes's spectacular photographs, we are proud to present the words and sentiments of Mariners Chairman and CEO John W. Ellis in his introductory memoir, and Frank Wetzel, a Puget Sound native, journalist, and writer who provided the main text. Also on the photographic front, we thank Ben VanHouten, Mariners photographer, for his contributions; Dave Aust of the Mariners for his work with the Mariners photo archives and production details; and the fine people at the Museum of History and Industry. The museum contains perhaps the finest collection of historic photographs that tell the story of baseball in the Puget Sound region, and they made it available to us.

Many others helped with this project over the two years. On the Mariners' side it was nurtured by club executives Randy Adamack and Bob Aylward, and former executive Paul Isaki. They constituted a management team to work with Hartley. Bill Johnson, vice president of the Rockey Company's Design Group, guided design and production, and copy editor Sherri Schultz and proofreader Miriam Bulmer applied their skills and knowledge of language to preparation of the text.

On behalf of the team—and speaking for Natalie Fobes and Frank Wetzel—the Mariners are particularly thankful for the cooperation of hundreds of men and women who built the ballpark and accommodated our requests for information and photo opportunities. This book would not have been possible without them, or the on-site supervisors for Hunt-Kiewit, general contractor, and the Public Facilities District. Foremost, we all are grateful for the commitment of the team owners, and their generosity.

All of us hope you will accept this book as a keepsake of a unique moment in professional sports history for Seattle, the Emerald City, and that you will spend many pleasurable hours reading about SAFECO Field.

Charles G. Armstrong
President, Seattle Mariners

CONTENTS

Hiroshi Yamauchi, president of
Nintendo Co. Ltd. of Kyoto,
Japan, and principal owner of the
Seattle Mariners.

To all the people of the Pacific Northwest:

With the opening of SAFECO Field I feel the same happiness as I did more than seven years ago. That was when I assured political leaders of the state of Washington and the people of the Pacific Northwest that I would do what I could financially to keep the Mariners in Seattle. I was joined in that endeavor by other civic-minded owners who had the same objective, and still do.

I share your pride in the opening of this magnificent ballpark. My wish is that you—as well as future generations of baseball fans—enjoy major-league baseball outdoors in the beautiful Pacific Northwest.

Hiroshi Yamauchi

Fred Hutchinson, shown in 1938 during his only season as a Rainiers player, had a distinguished major-league career as pitcher and manager.

The Last Time We Played on Real Grass

By John W. Ellis

I grew up in Seattle. We lived out near Seward Park. My two older brothers and I went to John Muir Elementary School and Franklin High School. Until World War II came, when both my brothers left and only one came back, it was a wonderful time to grow up.

We played baseball and football in the vacant lots, built tree houses, swam, rowed, sailed, skied, and fished. And then, about age 9, my life changed forever. I discovered the Seattle Rainiers, Sicks' Seattle Stadium, and baseball played on real grass. This adventure, as with so many personal stories about baseball, weaves in and out with memories of family, the players, and the place where they played. I soaked it all up.

The story of Sicks' Stadium, as I heard it much later, goes that one day at a National Brewers Convention in 1937, Emil Sick, who owned the Rainier brewery in Seattle, fell into conversation with Colonel Jacob Ruppert, who owned the New York Yankees as well as a few breweries. "Emil," the colonel said, "you ought to buy a baseball team." "Jacob," the Seattle brewer said, "that is

the greatest idea since Repeal." Sick bought the club and built a grand baseball park in Rainier Valley on the corner of Rainier Avenue and McClellan Street, where Eagle Hardware is today.

The property, which had previously been the site of Dugdale Field, was at the time a vacant lot. (Daniel E. Dugdale had owned the baseball team early in the 1900s.)

Neighbors would pasture an occasional horse on it. The land was surrounded on two sides by vegetable gardens that ran up the hill to 30th Avenue on the east and to McClellan on the south.

The gardens were owned by the Vacca family, who ran Pre's Garden Patch, the produce market across Rainier Avenue. Later, after the stadium opened, Vacca's gardens became known as "tightwad hill" for the fans who would gather up there to watch the game, looking down over the left-field fence into the park. My best friend, Bud McCartney, lived on 30th and you could watch the game from his front porch. I always thought he was the luckiest guy in the world.

ELLIS FAMILY

The "Baby Rainiers" youth team of a bygone day included John W. Ellis, second from right. Johnny Arnold is holding bat on left, and Frans Schack is holding bat on right. Others, from left: Kenneth Barr, Franklin Couch, Kendall DuPuy, Noel Travers, Donald Hoke, Ellis and Neal Barr.

The stadium was laid out with home plate facing southeast (home plate at SAFECO Field faces northeast) and the left- and right-field foul lines running east and south. It was in every way a classic ball field, seating about 14,000 in 6,000 grandstand seats, 2,000 box seats, and 6,200 bleacher seats. It cost more than $350,000 to build. Many considered it to be the finest minor-

league park in baseball.

In those days there were no major-league teams west of Chicago and St. Louis. The closest thing to the big leagues for those of us on the far West Coast was the AAA Pacific Coast League. All the big cities up and down the coast were represented, and some of the best players in baseball at the time, in or out of the major leagues, came to Seattle on a regular basis.

The stadium opened on June 15, 1938. Eighteen-year-old Freddy Hutchinson (known to all of us then and later as "Hutch"), right out of Franklin High School, pitched the second game and won it.

A couple of months later, on August 12, Hutch was again slated to start. It was his 19th birthday. I was there, a 9-year-old kid with some of the boys from my class at John Muir Grade School. What a celebration!

A crowd of 16,354 filled the seats. Hundreds of other fans stood five and six deep in the roped-off areas along the outfield fences. Hutch being Hutch, he beat the San Francisco Seals, 3-2, with a five-hitter.

The golden era of Seattle baseball had begun. We started off by winning three straight pennants, ultimately winning a total of six. The Rainiers led all minor-league teams in attendance over the next 15 years. Seattle proved it was a baseball town second to none.

To a 9-year-old kid, Sicks' Stadium was truly a wondrous place. You entered at ground level. Inside, flanking the entry, were refreshment stands and souvenir booths, while in front were the stairs leading up to the field concourse. As you climbed to the top of the stairs your first view was of the field, with the infield in the foreground: green grass

Emil Sick

ringed by the brown of the base paths and dotted in the middle with the pitcher's mound. Then you saw an ocean of grass that seemed to stretch endlessly out to the fences. "How could anyone possibly hit a ball clear out there?" you'd wonder.

The concourse ran all the way around the grandstand and was intersected by a series of aisles, which led down to the box seats and up into the grandstand. Once you reached that concourse, nothing interrupted your view. It was almost as if you were on the field itself, and it didn't take much to imagine you were in the game. At that age, fantasy is life. The box seats were actually steel folding chairs, eight to a box, like the kind you would use with a card table. A pipe rail enclosed each box. When my dad pointed out Mr. Sick's box to me, I couldn't have been more impressed if I had seen the king of England, who was a big figure in those days.

A lot of my memories of Sicks' Stadium include my dad. We usually would sit in the grandstand, although I can remember Dad arranging to let us sit in someone's box seats once in a while. When we kids went without Dad, it was always the bleachers. Not only was the price right, but you had lots of room to horse around

with your buddies.

The grandstands were covered, the front box seats relatively unprotected, and the bleachers completely open. Frequently, when a typical sputtering Seattle shower would interrupt play, the gates to the grandstand would be opened to let us fill in the vacant grandstand seats.

Memories come flooding back. Magical August days with a

Sicks' Seattle Stadium at the corner of Rainier Avenue and McClellan, now the site of a large retail center.

warm north breeze and Mount Rainier perched over right field. Cold, clammy nights huddled under blankets watching the drizzle reflect off the lights. Legend is that the stadium was a pitcher's park in the spring and the fall because of the heavy moist air, but that it became a hitter's park in the summer when the air warmed up and the afternoon breeze blew.

Baseball on our field was a kaleidoscopic blend of colors, sounds, and smells. Bright green

grass merged into the darker green of the outfield fences, which were spattered with color from the signs that dotted them. The American flag towered over the center-field scoreboard, and you could even see the guy who worked the board looking out his window at the game. On holidays, bright pennants and bunting decorated the stadium inside and out.

The sounds were so special: the crack of a bat, the *pop* a fastball made as it hit the catcher's glove, the distinctive calls of the

umpire—"Steee-ryke," "Yeer-r-r out"—catcalls from fans, the chatter of the players, the public-address announcer, who sounded to me like the announcer on "The March of Time," a brief news segment shown in movie theaters.

And the ever-present smells. Of the grass: freshly mown on a sunny summer Sunday afternoon, or damp and pungent on a misty spring evening. Of the food: hot dogs brought around by a man with a fragrantly steaming kettle in

his basket. He'd pull yours out of the kettle, put it on a bun, lather it up with your choice of mustard or relish, and pass it down to you.

We ate peanuts, bags and bags of them. There was always some show-offy young kid who liked to imitate the voice of the hawkers and transpose their words: "Pea corn, pop nuts, chewing water, and soda gum!"

The stadium was where *our* heroes plied their trade—not someone else's heroes like DiMaggio or Gehrig, but *our* heroes. Players like Edo Vanni, another local kid like Hutch and a heck of a player who went on to manage the team. There was lanky Bill Lawrence covering center field; Jo Jo White stealing another base; Big Mike Hunt parking one over the fence; Dick Gyselman never flinching at the bullet down the line; Hal Turpin, a marvelous pitcher; Dick "Kewpie" Barrett, probably our best of all time; and always, on any list, Hutch.

It is remarkable that Hutch, who played for Seattle only one season and did not come back to manage the team until 1955 (and then for only one full and one half season), left such a lasting impact. I guess it had something to do with what we thought a ballplayer/hero should be: strong, loyal, determined to win, a team player who stood up for the other players. And I'm sure part of it came from the fact that he was *our* guy—from Seattle—from a well-known Seattle family. Of course, it did not hurt that he had quite a distinguished pitching career for 10 years with the Detroit Tigers, and then managed the Tigers, the St. Louis Cardinals, and the Cincinnati Reds.

Cancer cut Hutch down in the prime of life on November 12, 1964. These many years later, it is such a thrill to see Hutch honored through the lifesaving work of the Fred Hutchinson Cancer Research Center, which was founded by Bill Hutchinson in memory of his brother.

All of the stadium's sights, sounds, and smells were tied together by a voice that spoke baseball to me and the rest of us fans: Leo Lassen. Lazy Sunday afternoons would be spent listening to Leo as he described every intimate detail of the game. He'd conjure up images of Dick "Kewpie" Barrett reaching for the rosin bag one more time as the count went to 3 and 2; of Mount Rainier looming over the right-field fence "like a big strawberry ice cream cone"; of what it felt like to be hit in the foot by a foul tip: "You don't know what you've missed if you've never been . . .";

The Vacca family owned vegetable gardens on two sides of Sicks' Stadium, and ran a produce market called Pre's Garden Patch across Rainier Avenue.

"Back, back, and it's over"; "Oh baby, that was a lulu." And so was he.

At our house, if the team was playing, the radio was on and Leo was there making it real. I venture that there are very few players from that era in Seattle who are better remembered than Leo. And I believe the same will be true of Dave Niehaus for this generation.

The most special moments of baseball for this child, and later for this adult, occurred with my dad. Baseball was one of the few experiences we were able to share as equals. He loved the game; he'd even played some at the college level. Although he was a busy guy, he always had time to take me to games, often taking some friends of mine along as well. He kept score diligently. Dad was a real fan and he took the game seriously. He believed in supporting his team, even in bad times. I can remember how irritated he'd get if a player was booed, even a player on the other team. It was very important to win, but more important to play hard, do your best, and always be a good sport.

After I grew up and left home to start a family of my own, my baseball ties with my dad continued. Invariably during the season, the team would be part of our discussions. What did I think of the new left-hander? Did he like the new manager?

One of my fondest memories of my dad involves baseball. On a Sunday afternoon a year or so before his death, I took him on a sail across Puget Sound, just the two of us. The Mariners were playing out of town. We anchored in Port Madison to have lunch. It was a glorious sunny day, as only a summer day in this region can be. We sat in the cockpit, the waters lapping at the hull, and listened to the ball game. As the game ended and we raised anchor to sail back home, he said to me, "John, this has to be just about as close to heaven as you can get in this world."

In recent years I have found myself another piece of heaven with involvement in baseball to an extent I'd never dreamed. During my time as chairman and CEO of the Mariners, starting in 1992, I have watched the reawakening of the love of baseball in this community, which was so strong in those early days. The remarkable efforts of a dedicated local ownership, a strong commitment from the political, business, and labor communities, and most of all the overwhelming fan support have come together to make the dream of our new grass ball field a reality. The SAFECO Field story is told for all of them.

My story is part of a continuum. Our children and their children have grown to love this game, and they will grow to love their new grass field as much as our generation loved ours. I believe that, as time passes, although their memories of scores and players and seasons will fade, they will always remember those who shared that love with them. And after all, isn't that finally what it's all about: a gift from one generation to another.

. . . .

On game day in 1964, Sicks' Stadium was full of fans, often a familiar sight during the years of the Seattle Rainiers. Seating capacity was more than 14,000.

The most memorable moment in Mariners' history: a grinning Ken Griffey Jr., at home plate, seconds after scoring the winning run to beat the Yankees, 6-5, in the 1995 American League playoffs.

Members of the Mariners ownership group gathered with Ken Griffey Jr. to take a ceremonial scoop of ground at the home plate site. (March 1997)

Ken Griffey Jr. made a special trip from spring training to welcome the nearly 30,000 who came to the ballpark site for ground-breaking ceremonies. (March 1997)

Diamond in the Emerald City

Text by Frank Wetzel

Whoever wants to know the heart and mind of America, a scholar once famously said, had better learn baseball, the rules and reality of the game. For almost 150 years, since before the Civil War, baseball has reflected the dreams of America, and seldom more so than now. In these times of complexity, it provides simplicity. In these times of ambiguity, it provides certainty. In these times of chaos and separation, it provides order and community.

It's easy to make too much of baseball, of course. It is, after all, only a game, best watched while forgetting the burdens of life, "a wonderful waste of time," said a writer, "a raspberry in the face of authority."

Still, baseball can excite and unite a community, as the Mariners excited and united the Pacific Northwest in 1995. And from life's sweet moments often come added delights. In this instance the thrill of victory in 1995 led to a new ballpark for the Pacific Northwest and the

Seattle Mariners. Some would suggest it led to a ballpark— SAFECO Field—that is the best in baseball.

Through the wonders of hindsight, it's possible to know with precision the exact moment that construction of a new ballpark in Seattle was predetermined. The date was August 24, 1995. It's the bottom of the ninth inning and the score is tied at 7 against New York. The Yankees' reliever, John Wetteland, tries to sneak a fastball inside against Ken Griffey Jr. *Whammo!* The ball hits the foul pole. The Mariners win, 9-7.

But wait a minute. There's more to the story than a swing of Griffey's bat. It wasn't widely recognized at the time, but Mariners fans were given an inkling of victory as early as 1994, the year before Griffey struck the precipitating smash. That year the Mariners won 10 of their final 11 games. When the season ended, they were baseball's hottest team. Sadly, play stopped six weeks early, on August 11, the

5

Tower cranes rise from the rubble of the last warehouse demolished to make way for the ballpark. (July 1997)

PUBLIC FACILITIES DISTRICT

Ballpark "footprint" noted on aerial taken in February 1997, before construction began.

BEN VANHOUTEN

A section of a tower crane is "flown" into place. These cranes lift and move materials and equipment around a construction site. At one point two of the tallest tower cranes on the West Coast were being used to construct the ballpark. (July 1997)

season cut short by a strike.

The Mariners' manager, Lou Piniella, saw the promise. In September 1994 he lamented, "I would venture to say if baseball were still being played, we'd be preparing for the playoffs right now." That appraisal seems realistic. The Mariners had put together a 10-1 streak while on an endless road trip, forced out of the Kingdome by falling roof tiles.

The strike delayed the start of the 1995 season. But the Mariners' first game, on April 27, left fans in the crowd smacking their lips. Griffey, the Mariners' redoubtable center fielder, smashed a three-run homer into the Kingdome's third deck. Pitcher Randy Johnson, on his way to a stunning 18-2 season,

combined with relievers Bill Risley and Bobby Ayala for a 3-0 victory over the Detroit Tigers. It was the first opening-day shutout in Mariners history.

Despite its auspicious beginning, though, the season of '95 was not to be a cakewalk. On May 26, Griffey, making yet another of his spectacular catches, fractured two bones in his left wrist. The manager of the Baltimore Orioles, Phil Regan, called Griffey's grab "probably the greatest catch I've ever seen." Tim Egan, writing for the *New York Times*, gazed four months into the future and dreamed: "It's mid-September, the Mariners are in a pennant race, and the new stadium will be voted on any day. Then, back in center field after a

summer of convalescence is Junior. He's batting cleanup, in more ways than he could ever know."

Egan was speaking figuratively—Griffey doesn't bat in the cleanup position—but his prediction was not far off. Griffey missed 73 games, not returning to the lineup until August 15. By then, the struggling Mariners, dreadfully missing Griffey, were 12 1/2 games behind the California Angels. His return did not immediately rejuvenate the team; the next week they lost four of five games, putting their season's record at 54-55.

A players-only meeting on August 24, preceding a game with New York, at first seemed to provide no additional inspiration.

But then the magic started. It went like this: Down 7-6 with two outs in the bottom of the ninth. No one on base. Vince Coleman walks. He steals second. He steals third! Tony Fernandez, the New York shortstop, fails to catch Joey Cora's soft liner. Coleman scores! The game is tied at 7.

The presence of the fleet Coleman in the Mariners' lineup reflected the team's new optimism. He was added on August 15, two weeks after the Mariners acquired pitcher Andy Benes. They were the first players the Mariners ever added during the second half of the season to support a pennant-race situation.

Up to bat comes Griffey, wrist healed but still sore. The Yankee

7

closer, John Wetteland, tries to muscle a fastball inside. Big mistake. Griffey knows upon impact that he has hit a home run, this one bouncing off the foul pole. Fly, fly away! Clear through the 1998 season, this was Griffey's only game-winning homer. "That was the one that got us going," Piniella declared. "It wasn't just how we did it, but because Junior did it. We had him back." That glorious victory propelled the Mariners to a 25-11 completion of the season.

Mariners fans, so often disappointed, were slow to realize what was happening. In mid-September only 12,102 turned out for a game with Minnesota. But on September 22, when Seattle beat Oakland and at last moved ahead of faltering California into first place, 51,550 turned out. Paid attendance at the final 12 games, including the postseason, averaged 54,045. The fans took over the Kingdome as the Mariners took over the Pacific Northwest. The Mariners' story even captured the attention of fans across the country.

Only a week before the regular season ended, the Mariners were one game behind California for first place in the American League West. They made up the deficit and played a sudden-death game for the title in the Kingdome on Monday, October 2, the Mariners' first-ever extended-season game. The Mariners wrapped up the game in the seventh inning when shortstop Luis Sojo hit a broken-bat, bases-loaded double, the ball lodging under the visitors' bullpen bench.

Four runs scored, as announcer Rick Rizzs proclaimed, "Everybody scores!" Randy Johnson, the Big Unit, was seldom bigger. He pitched a complete game, giving up only three hits in the 9-1 win.

Johnson gave Mariners fans credit for inspiring him. Tom Verducci, writing about Seattle's phenomenal season for *Sports Illustrated*, quoted him: "I guarantee you, if the fans hadn't come out in the numbers they did and been as loud as they were, we would not have accomplished what we did. I know whenever I was getting tired and I heard them chanting, 'Ran-dee! Ran-dee!,' I motivated myself to a level I otherwise wouldn't have reached."

After beating California and winning the West, Seattle faced the New York Yankees in the Division Series. The Mariners lost the first two games in New York, 9-6 and 7-5, before returning to Seattle. Had they lost one more game, their season would have been over. But Johnson held New York to six hits as the Mariners won Game 3, 7-4. They scored five runs in the eighth inning of Game 4, winning 11-8, once again coming from behind. It was becoming a habit; they overtook opponents 43 times during the season, including 12 times during September. The series was tied at two games each. The Division Series hinged on the remaining game.

The Yankees started their ace pitcher, David Cone. New York took early leads of 2-1 and 4-2. But the Mariners scored twice in the eighth inning to tie the score

8

Rows of pilings stand like sentinels against the evening sky. Throughout the summer of 1997,
the earth shook and the air reverberated as more than 1,450 pilings were driven into the ground. (June 1997)

9

at 4. Neither team scored in the ninth, and the game went into extra innings.

Increasing the drama, Jack McDowell, like Cone a past winner of the Cy Young Award as the league's best pitcher, relieved Cone for New York. In the top of the 11th inning, the Yankees scored once for a 5-4 lead. Fans winced. Three more outs and the Mariners were finished.

Verducci, capturing the next moments for *Sports Illustrated*,

An ironworker climbs a partially assembled tower crane.
A total of four tower cranes were needed to build the ballpark. (July 1997)

May 1997: First tower crane on site.
First piles driven. Warehouse demolition continues.

wrote, "Finally, with two runners on in the 11th, Edgar Martinez smashed a pitch into the leftfield corner. Cora scored easily from third, and Griffey, with unprecedented haste, did likewise from first with the winning run.

Fireworks burst and a great, joyous noise fairly shook the walls of the huge concrete cavern . . ."

Final score: Seattle 6, New York 5. Johnson won the game for Seattle in relief, pitching with one day's rest, striking out six in

three innings. It was a superb performance by two of baseball's best pitchers.

There followed a celebration of magnificent proportions— not just by the 57,411 fans in the Kingdome but throughout the

Northwest. People hollered from their windows, banged on pots and pans, honked their horns, capitalized on the occasion to propose marriage, exclaimed repeatedly to strangers, "How about them M's?" The 240-point head-

Cranes and pilings are reflected in the lenses of ironworker Keith Weldon's safety glasses. Many workers, including Keith, said they were proud to be involved in the building of the new ballpark. (July 1997)

Dwarfed by the Kingdome, a worker prepares to unload iron reinforcing bar, or rebar, from a truck. (August 1997)

line in the *Seattle Post-Intelligencer*, M'S DO IT!, was the newspaper's biggest since World War II.

Two days later, the Mariners played Cleveland for the American League championship in a best-of-seven series. A surprise starter, 21-year-old rookie Bob Wolcott, won the first game for the Mariners, 3-2. Cleveland won the second, 5-2, but Seattle took the third, also 5-2, behind the four-hit pitching of Johnson. That, alas, was Seattle's final

Dave "Cowboy" Stezaker, Jerry Anderson, and Bobby Birkeland, left to right, set rebar cages on top of pilings already in the ground. The cages, encased in concrete, became part of the hefty foundation supporting the massive roof and grandstands. (August 1997)

thrust. Cleveland captured the championship by winning the last three games, 7-0, 3-2, and 4-0.

In the clubhouse after the last game, John Ellis, chairman and chief executive officer of the club, thanked the team for a splendid season. Piniella extended his own thanks. The players listened appreciatively to Ellis and Piniella, but they also heard the sustained applause still rolling from the grandstands. At Piniella's suggestion, the Mariners—some without complete uniforms, some with ice bags taped to aching bodies—walked back to the field. The fans were still yelling and clapping, 15 minutes after the game had ended, for a team that had just lost the league championship. Some of the players, touched by fans' support, wept.

A budding affair had blossomed. The Northwest had fallen in love.

Still, in the middle of the Mariners' stirring run for the championship, major-league baseball in Seattle sustained a ringing

With the ballpark site covering 19.59 acres, a bicycle comes in handy. (July 1997)

A worker checks plans against the reality of a partially constructed wall. (July 1997)

defeat that did not appear in the box scores. On September 19, King County voters turned down a proposal to increase the sales tax by one-tenth of 1 percent to both finance a new ballpark and rejuvenate the Kingdome. The measure lost by only 1,082 votes of 491,918 cast.

Because of the momentum for approval provided by the Mariners' late-season drive, conventional wisdom held that if the election had occurred even one day later, the measure would have passed. Conventional wisdom also held that the defeat was ultimately for the best, because subsequently a financing plan that did not depend heavily on a sales tax, but relied on user taxes instead, was approved by the Washington State Legislature.

Before looking back at how the ballpark came to be, let's return to that earlier statement that SAFECO Field may be the best baseball park anywhere. How so?

First of all, it's the only outdoor park with a retractable roof. Presently only two other major-league ballparks have such roofs:

Inspector Tom Maddock checks the placement of rebar, designed to strengthen concrete, in the footings of the south runway. (July 1997)

Patrick Connor III cleans rebar after the concrete pour for the south runway. The pour was the biggest on site and took seven hours. (August 1997)

Willie Bullard is splattered with concrete as he mans the
hose on the end of a boom attached to the concrete pump.
Over 700 cubic yards of concrete were poured into this section
of the south runway foundation. It has to be strong—this structure
supports not only part of the grandstand but also half
of the weight of the retractable roof. (August 1997)

Toronto and Phoenix. But both are high-walled indoor parks whose roofs can be opened somewhat incidentally, much like an automobile sunroof.

SAFECO Field, by contrast, is like a convertible car whose top is fully down 95 percent of the time, with the side windows always open. Mariners fans are outdoors, whether the roof is open or closed.

Parks currently under development in Milwaukee and Houston will have retractable roofs, too. But they will also be indoor parks: Milwaukee's because of the cold, Houston's because of the heat. Mariners fans may be chilly in the early spring and late fall, but Northwesterners famously know how to dress for clammy weather. They will bring sweaters and blankets to SAFECO Field as needed. And they will stay dry.

Second: George Will—the syndicated columnist and author, and also a stalwart baseball fan—has declared that the three most important developments in baseball since World War II were Jackie Robinson's breaking the

Workers prepare a column form and beam in right field. At summer's end
the lower levels of the grandstand began to take shape. (August 1997)

Steve Kreifels checks plans in the underground batting area. Plans were
complex enough to be measured in weight as well as pages. (August 1997)

race barrier, free agency, and the construction of Camden Yards, Baltimore's ballpark. Since Camden, handsome ballparks have been built in Atlanta, Cleveland, Arlington near Dallas, and Denver. In a happy convergence, Seattle has drawn from each—learned from their strengths and shortcomings—and incorporated the best aspects of the new generation of ballparks in the design of SAFECO Field.

The best in those other cities happened to be a return to tradition. By design, the new parks look old. They are modeled on venerable parks such as Crosley Field in Cincinnati, built in 1912, conveniently reached by trolley and shaped by its urban setting; Shibe Park in Philadelphia, built in 1909, featuring a brick facade and graceful home-plate entry; and Ebbets Field in Brooklyn, with its repetitive arches and archetypal entry. But the new parks, while looking traditional, retain the convenience of modern construction in such elements as their elevators and escalators, their direct sight lines, and the lightness permitted by steel rather than concrete construction. The architects of SAFECO Field absorbed those characteristics, burnished them, and transformed them into something uniquely Northwestern.

That's the third point: ballpark

"Going vertical" is an exciting time. It means the structure soon will begin to take shape. (July 1997)

A section of one of four tower cranes is hoisted into place along First Avenue. (July 1997)

Carpenters Tom Bartlett and Susan Showalter finish the forms for the first column.

planners captured the distinctive flavor of the region. Witness the many special touches: The extensive, tasteful artwork. The park's smooth congruency with the red bricks and window arches of nearby Pioneer Square. The panoramic views of downtown Seattle and Elliott Bay and the Olympics far beyond. The flavor of Pike Place Market at the concession stands. And the lacy filigree of the superstructure—all these are singularly, superbly Northwestern.

Brad Schrock, the chief designer of Denver's Coors Field, acted as a consultant for the Mariners at SAFECO Field. Because this ballpark's builders and backers have not deviated from their original high goals, "this ballpark clearly set a new standard in lots of ways," Schrock noted. "This field takes what's been done in Coors and Camden, which people said set standards, and elevates them a notch."

September 1997: Construction of columns, south runway walls.

An ironworker stretches to reach a piece of rebar. "Rod busters" tied countless lengths of rebar into mats designed to strengthen concrete walls. (September 1997)

Keith Floyd places rebar into a beam form on the concourse level of the ballpark. (August 1997)

Framed by a doorway, a worker erects scaffolding supports on the ground level under the Hit It Here Cafe. (October 1997)

Carpenter Norm Westerfeld takes a break from his work on an air intake at the ballpark. (September 1997)

Ironworker apprentice April Finkbonner grimaces as she pulls taut the wire connecting rebar on a wall. More than 19 percent of the workers on site were apprentices, eclipsing the goal of 15 percent. (September 1997)

Columnist Will has suggested that baseball teams reflect the character of their home cities. Perhaps. But more often true is that ballparks reflect the cities where they are sited. More than any other ballpark, SAFECO Field reflects its environs. It's a handsome fit.

Further, it comes at a time of great general renaissance in Seattle. A new art museum, a newer symphony hall, a new central library (and branch libraries, too) and new courthouses soon to be built, a glistening and rejuve-nated downtown retail area—and, coming up soon near SAFECO Field, a new football stadium and exhibition hall. Art, music, literature, law, commerce, sports: it's a vital and vigorous period in the development of a great city.

The Heroes and Saviors in a Century of Baseball

Baseball has been part of Seattle's texture almost since the territorial legislature granted a city charter in 1869. By coincidence, that was the year the Cincinnati Red Stockings made a barnstorming tour of the West Coast, the first visit by a professional team to the West.

Bill O'Neal's book *The Pacific Coast League, 1903–1988* describes the context of those times. In its early days, Seattle was a member of the Class C Pacific Northwest League and its team played at the YMCA park at 12th Avenue and Jefferson Street. In 1903, the Seattle Indians joined San Francisco, Los Angeles, Oakland, Sacramento, and Portland in the Pacific Coast League.

In those days, teams played 200 games per season, and a season ran eight months or longer. Each team had only 14 or 15 players, but they were paid as well as major leaguers. Travel was minimized by playing seven consecutive games against one opponent, with two weeks at home and two weeks on the road. Admission was two bits—25 cents. Ballparks had only one dressing room, so visiting teams pulled on their flannel uniforms in

Construction workers make concrete forms out of rebar. (September 1997)

Ironworkers John Roark and Enola Thomas tie a reinforcing steel bar mat for the concourse level's concrete floor. Enola says it is not her back but her knees that ache at the end of the day. (October 1997)

21

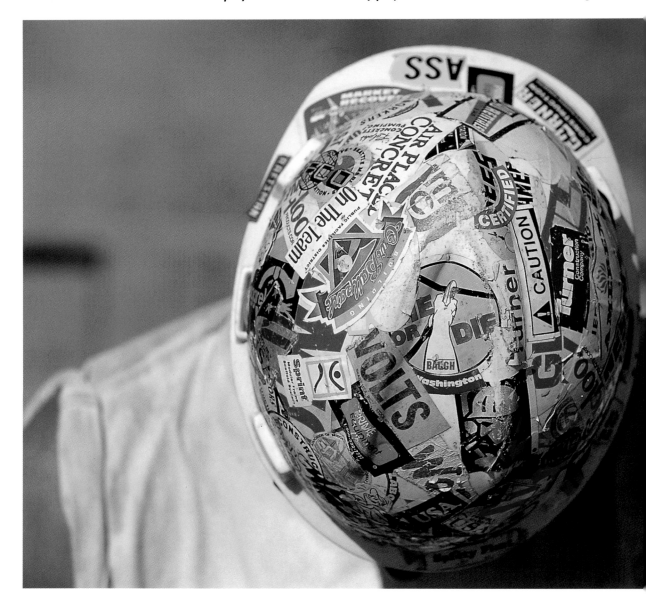

their hotel rooms.

There was no dawdling; in 1905 Los Angeles and Oakland played a doubleheader in slightly more than an hour and a half. The first game took 47½ minutes, the second 51 minutes. Both games went nine innings.

Playing surfaces were rough and gloves were small. In 1903, in a game with Seattle, Oakland committed 15 errors. During early games of the PCL, there was only one umpire; a second was added in 1908. Jack McCarthy was the first umpire to wear a chest protector. It soon became a common part of the equipment for catchers, who previously had to position themselves far behind the plate, making base stealing easy.

Seattle dropped out of the Pacific Coast League after 1906, playing in the Class B Northwest League from 1907 to 1917, but rejoined the PCL in 1918.

Dugdale Field, a high-quality park with 15,000 seats, was built in Seattle at Rainier Avenue and McClellan Street in 1913. It burned on July 4, 1932, and the Indians moved to Civic Stadium (now called Memorial Stadium, at Seattle Center) for six years.

In 1938 Emil Sick bought the team for $200,000 and built Sicks' Seattle Stadium on the site of the old Dugdale Field, ushering in Seattle's golden PCL years. The Rainiers, as they were then called, grabbed Fred Hutchinson, an 18-year-old pitcher, as he came out of Franklin High School in Seattle. He led the 1938 team with a record of 25-7 and an earned run average of 2.48, the best in the league. Not only that, he hit .313. Although the Rainiers soon sold Hutchinson to the Detroit Tigers, they made the playoffs for six consecutive seasons, winning pennants in 1939, 1940, and 1942.

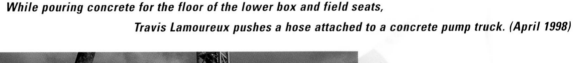

**While pouring concrete for the floor of the lower box and field seats,
Travis Lamoureux pushes a hose attached to a concrete pump truck. (April 1998)**

**Finishers swiftly smooth the freshly poured concrete
on the First Avenue concourse level. (March 1998)**

**Careful with the details, a concrete
finisher puts the final touches on a new sidewalk
near the main entrance. (March 1998)**

Those were the days when Leo Lassen was broadcasting Seattle's games, recreating road games from bare-bones Western Union reports. His nasal descriptions of home runs—"Back, back, and it's over!"—were as well known then as Dave Niehaus's "Fly, fly away!" is today.

In the '30s, players were not rushed to the major leagues. In Joe DiMaggio's first full season with San Francisco, for example, he hit in 61 consecutive games—his mark of 56 consecutive games still stands as the major-league record—and batted .340. The Yankees purchased him for $25,000 but left him in San Francisco for another year of seasoning. That year he hit .398 with 34 home runs. Many Hall of Famers came up but were not rushed up through the PCL: Ted Williams, Tony Lazzeri, Mickey Cochrane, Paul Waner, Lefty

A form for a wall is "flown" over plumbers Steve Fuhrman (left) and
Steve Johnson as they set sleeves for plumbing. The holes for the mechanical systems
had to be installed in the walls before the concrete was poured. (November 1997)

November 1997: Construction progresses from southeast corner.
Concrete support beams for seating area poured.

O'Doul, Ernie Lombardi, and Frank Crosetti among them.

A local favorite for many years was Dick "Kewpie" Barrett, a ruddy-cheeked right-hander who pitched for Seattle from 1935 to 1942 and again from 1947 to 1949. Starting in 1935, he won 20 or more games in seven of the next eight seasons. He was nearly matched by Hal Turpin, who pitched for Seattle from 1937 through 1945, winning 20 or more games four years in a row and maintaining an ERA below 3.00. Other favorites were Dick Gyselman, a fixture at third base from 1935 to 1944; shortstop Alan Strange; second baseman Fred Muller; first baseman George Archie; and outfielders Edo Vanni,

Jo Jo White, Jungle Jim Rivera, Bill Lawrence, and Art Hunt. Team rosters were stable, and players had long careers. Barrett won 325 games in the minors, including 234 in the PCL. Sad Sam Gibson won 20 games six times for the San Francisco Seals and was still pitching in the Georgia–Alabama league at age 50. Another former PCL player, Luke Easter, played professional ball until he was 49.

Minor-league attendance plunged in 1951, O'Neal wrote, because of television, Little Leagues, and home air conditioning. The demise of the PCL as a strong independent league came when Walter O'Malley of the Brooklyn Dodgers bought the

ballpark in Los Angeles and Horace Stoneham of the New York Giants began maneuvers to take the Giants to San Francisco. The National League granted permission for both moves on May 28, 1957.

Seattle's last year in the PCL was 1968; the next year, the city was awarded an expansion franchise in the American League. But sadly, after playing only one season, Seattle's first major-league team, the Pilots, departed for Milwaukee.

Seattle and the state sued Major League Baseball for damages of $32.5 million. Slade Gorton, the incoming state attorney general, led the effort. For two years Seattle was without

A rare winter sun casts long shadows as a worker climbs down a ladder from the south concourse before leaving for the Thanksgiving holiday, a much-needed break. Many of the workers put in 12-hour days, six days a week, for months. (November 1997)

Norm Westerfeld catches a tool to connect two rebar panels.

A hazy December sun silhouettes rebar columns and carpenters. (December 1997)

organized professional baseball. Then a team played five seasons in the Class A Northwest League.

The American League readmitted Seattle and settled the suit in 1976, when it expanded from 12 to 14 teams. The Toronto Blue Jays came in at the same time. This time the Seattle team was named the Mariners and was principally owned by Les Smith, a broadcaster from Portland and Seattle, and Danny Kaye, the Hollywood entertainer. Four Seattle businessmen—Stan Golub, Walter Schoenfeld, Jim Walsh, and Jim Stillwell—were minor stockholders, although Walsh and Stillwell soon sold. Lou Gorman was the front-office boss and Darrell Johnson was the field manager.

The team played its first game in the new Kingdome in 1977 before 57,762 spectators, losing to the Angels. The first year's attendance totaled 1,388,511, far more than expected. But that figure shrank by half a million in 1978, thanks in part to the distraction of the SuperSonics, Seattle's professional basketball team, who reached the NBA finals that year and won the NBA championship in 1979. Attendance dropped steadily to 636,276 by 1981 (a strike-shortened season) before beginning an irregular trend upward. By that year Smith, a truly nice guy, and Kaye, a very funny guy, had sold the team for $11 million to George Argyros.

Argyros had two strikes against him before he set foot in Seattle. First, he was a real estate developer. Broad-minded Northwesterners might have forgiven him that but,

second, he was from California. Argyros never had a chance. He quickly became the local choice for the man you love to hate.

One of Argyros's achievements was bringing in two executives who are still with the club: Chuck Armstrong from his real estate company, who became president in October 1983, and William (Woody) Woodward, who became general manager in July 1988. Less than a year after joining the club, on May 25, Woodward made perhaps the best trade in Mariners history. He sent Mark Langston, who would become a free agent at the end of the season, to Montreal for two right-handed pitchers, Brian Holman and Gene Harris—and, oh yes, left-handed Randy Johnson. That same season, a 19-year-old outfielder also joined the Mariners: Ken Griffey Jr.

The Argyros ownership ended on August 22, 1989, when he sold the team for $77 million to Emmis Broadcasting Company of Indianapolis. There was a brief era of good feeling for the new owner, Jeff Smulyan. But Smulyan soon talked about moving the team—St. Petersburg–Tampa seemed to be his choice for a new location—and this naturally alienated local fans.

On the field the Mariners were starting to show promise. In 1990, Randy Johnson threw a no-hitter against the Detroit Tigers, winning 2-0. Later that season Ken Griffey Sr. joined the Mariners. He and Ken Griffey Jr. were the first father-son combination to play on the same major-league team.

Finally, in 1991, led by Griffey, Edgar Martinez, and second baseman Harold Reynolds, the Mariners compiled a winning season record for the first time—83-79. Attendance was a record 2,147,905. The successful season caused jubilation among fans and gave fresh hope for the future.

Despite a better team and higher attendance, Smulyan announced on December 6, 1991, that he would offer the club for sale to a local buyer. "It's not easy for me to tell you I have failed," Smulyan told a news conference. "This is a chance that gives the community the opportunity to take baseball into its heart, own it, care for it, and make it successful." Rumors spread immediately that Smulyan wished to take the ball club to Florida. Further speculation indicated there were no local buyers ready to step forward.

Smulyan's price for the Mariners: $100 million. Committees were formed in Seattle, and civic-minded people began the search for a savior. Top public officials in the city and state became active, including Governor Booth Gardner, King County Executive Tim Hill, and Mayor Norm Rice. Perhaps the most active was Senator Slade Gorton, who had been through the earlier "loss" of baseball in the Pacific Northwest.

Among his efforts, Gorton called on executives of Nintendo of America (NOA) to see what opportunities might exist. A world leader in video games, Nintendo employs some 1,000 people at its operations east of

Lake Washington. Specifically, the senator talked with Minoru Arakawa, president of NOA, and Howard Lincoln, then senior vice president of the company.

Lincoln, later to become chairman of NOA, remembers that one discussion included talk about problems that might be encountered with Major League Baseball over a Japanese owner. This activity, before the end of 1991, was to mark the beginning of a lengthy commitment by Lincoln to acquisition of the team, and then to the fortunes of the Mariners in succeeding years.

Arakawa and Lincoln agreed to see what could be done. Arakawa then called Hiroshi Yamauchi, president of Nintendo Co. Ltd. of Kyoto, Japan, and Arakawa's father-in-law, to tell him of the contact by Gorton and the concerns of leading public officials and citizens. Thankful for all the help that had been given to Nintendo of America by Puget Sound area people and NOA's success in North America, Yamauchi agreed to put up the entire $100 million if necessary. On Christmas Day, 1991, Arakawa and Lincoln called Gorton with the good news. Later it became known as an extraordinary Christmas present for the people of the Pacific Northwest.

The response was swift. Within a month, a group of investors was assembled and organized as The Baseball Club of Seattle, L.P. The prospective owners decided on a package of $100 million to buy the club and $25 million for operating capital, thereby starting the venture debt-free. Yamauchi

Lights from construction cranes glow in the early evening. (December 1997)

April 1998: South, north runway extensions in place over railroad tracks.
Seating risers poured. Structural steel for upper grandstand bowl placed.

Ironworker William Hernandez pounds bolts into place
on one of the first beams. Mike Moses joins other workers who
gather to watch and take photographs as the
"raising gang" maneuvers the first support of the north
runway into place. By this time, literally hundreds of people
have been involved in the design, engineering, and fabrication
of the iron. But it comes down to one man, Darren Pyle,
to put in the first bolt. (December 1997)

agreed to contribute $75 million, with the balance provided by other owners. The second-largest investment came from Christopher Larson, a Microsoft manager and one of the early employees of the software company. Others with Microsoft connections who have joined Larson are Rob Glaser, Jeffrey S. Raikes, Craig Watjen, Raymond B. "Buck" Ferguson, Carl Stork, and William Marklyn. Larson has

continued to play a major role in planning and strategic decisions by the owners group.

Other members of the ownership group include John McCaw, Rufus Lumry, and Wayne Perry, all formerly associated with McCaw Cellular; and Judith Bigelow.

To assure control of the prospective owners group by local Seattle people, Yamauchi turned over control of his interest to

Arakawa and Lincoln, as senior officers of NOA and Nintendo Co. Ltd. They both went on the seven-person board of directors, along with Larson, Watjen, and McCaw; Frank Shrontz, then chairman and chief executive officer of the Boeing Company; and John Ellis, then chairman and chief executive officer of Puget Sound Power & Light. Shrontz and Ellis were designated "community members" of the board,

representing people throughout the region.

The intention of The Baseball Club of Seattle to purchase the Mariners was announced at a press conference on January 23, 1992, at which top business and political leaders spoke of their happiness. Lincoln, who read a statement as spokesman for The Baseball Club of Seattle on behalf of Yamauchi, and Ellis, who had been chosen as chairman of the

group, spoke for ownership interests. Lincoln said the only motivation of Yamauchi "is to help this community." The press conference launched a nearly six-month effort, much of it carried out in national media, to acquire the Mariners. Ellis and Lincoln devoted countless hours to the quest, along with their other corporate duties.

The first response of Major League Baseball to the offer from local Seattle interests to purchase the Mariners was disappointing, and signaled just how difficult it would be to convince owners of other ball clubs and officials of baseball to accept the ownership group. Commissioner of Baseball Fay Vincent immediately expressed doubt that the offer would be approved, citing baseball's policy that investors must be "from North America." His response caused a national uproar

Huge concrete and steel raker beams will eventually support the Terrace Club area of the ballpark bowl. (January 1997)

Foreman Pete Coubertier talks with Jerry Marvin. (March 1998)

Carpenter foremen Greg Child and Susie Showalter share a radio to ask one
of the tower crane operators to "fly" in a pallet of wood. (November 1997)

in media across the nation. Key baseball club owners were less outspoken in their comments, but were no less difficult to convince.

After months of negotiation with Vincent and owners of other teams, the sale was approved in June 1992, and the new owners took over on July 1. As part of the agreement with Major League Baseball, Yamauchi agreed to take a passive role in governance of the team. In remarks at a press conference on June 12, Lincoln addressed the willingness of Yamauchi to take a lesser role in relationship to his dollar investment. "Quite frankly, I doubt that

baseball fans in the Pacific Northwest or elsewhere would expect any investor to risk $75 million under such conditions. However, Mr. Yamauchi promised Senator Gorton and Governor Gardner that he would help keep the Mariners in Seattle and he is a man of his word."

Lincoln also acknowledged the involvement of Senator Gorton. "I think it's fair to say that Senator

Gorton is the principal reason why the Seattle Mariners will remain in the Pacific Northwest." Ellis became the owners' representative, and chairman and CEO of the Mariners. With this, an important ingredient of the Mariners' future success—local ownership and management—was in place.

The Mariners had a disappointing 1992 season. They lost 98 games and finished last in the American League West despite a talented but young team. After the close of the 1992 season, however, the new ownership began to fulfill its commitment to bring competitive baseball to Seattle and take steps toward putting a better team on the field. Lou Piniella, one of baseball's most successful managers, was hired as field manager. Multi-year contracts were signed with Ken Griffey Jr., Edgar Martinez, and Chris Bosio. It was the first time the Mariners had ever had more than two players on long-term contracts. The player payroll, about $23 million in 1992, was increased the next year to $32 million.

The benefits were immediate. In 1993 the Mariners finished over .500 and home attendance topped two million. But despite the improvement on the field, the club lost nearly $17 million. "As we looked at it," Ellis observed, "it became apparent that no matter how well we did on the field, without a facility that was capable of producing significantly more revenue, we would forever be foreclosed from being competitive economically."

The first thought was to reno-

Greg Child diagrams a riser form on a piece of scrap wood for Eric Loschky. It took almost a year for the riser crew to build the concrete forms to support the grandstand seats. (November 1998)

Eric Loschky and Dan Slate wrestle with raker beam forms. After the concrete cures, the forms are stripped and used again. (November 1998)

vate the Kingdome. The Mariners' lease for the stadium was to expire at the end of the 1996 season. Hill, the King County executive, had spoken publicly of a willingness to negotiate a new long-term lease and make capital improvements in the Kingdome.

Studies by Coopers & Lybrand, an accounting firm, and HOK Sport, designers of ballparks including Camden Yards, concluded that changes in the Kingdome would not accomplish the goals of the Mariners, or any major-league baseball team using the facility. Multipurpose stadiums such as the Kingdome—the Seahawks of the National Football League also played there—were falling into disfavor everywhere; they weren't adequate for the needs of football *or* baseball.

Meanwhile, other cities were building handsome new ballparks exclusively for baseball, and fans were flocking to them. First was new Comiskey Park in Chicago. Then came Camden Yards in Baltimore, lauded as a breakthrough because of the way it was integrated with its surroundings and because of its use of structural steel instead of concrete. Jacobs Field in Cleveland and Coors Field in Denver followed Baltimore's lead in the use of steel. Since completion of the parks, sellout crowds have been the norm there.

"Our objective in taking over the team," explained Ellis, "was to ensure the long-term future of professional baseball here in this city. And ultimately one of the ways of making that happen was

to come up with a new facility."

By the end of 1993, the Mariners made the possibility of a new ballpark their first priority, and they put Paul Isaki, vice president of business development, in charge of the project. Isaki, a longtime Mariners fan, joined the staff in 1992 after eight years with Governor Booth Gardner, the last three years as director of the Department of Trade and Economic Development. (In April of 1999, the ballpark all but completed, Isaki rejoined state government, accepting appointment as Governor Gary Locke's special trade representative.) In his job with Governor Gardner, Isaki worked extensively with projects that often combined public and private initiatives. As it turned out, his was just the sort of experience the Mariners needed.

In 1993 it became obvious to management that the club needed a new ballpark. But that was a long-term goal, perhaps seven to ten years in the future. "At the start," Isaki recalled, "it was the kind of subject that we talked about only to our close associates because nobody else would believe we had the audacity to even ask, let alone give it a try."

Had Seattle voters not approved and built the Kingdome years earlier, Isaki noted, major-league baseball would not have returned to Seattle. Still, the Dome came to mean "something you could play baseball in, but it wasn't an environment that either showed off the game to its best effect or encouraged the community to really embrace the team or the sport." But with an improved

An ironworker directs a crane operator as a section of iron is flown into place. Piece by piece, the north runway took shape through the winter. (December 1997)

As the cold and rainy winter dragged on, workers built the structural supports for the upper-level seats. (February 1998)

Spreading holiday cheer, Robi Herbert hangs a Christmas wreath on the Herrick construction trailer where her husband works. (December 1997)

A worker walks across the tip of the south roof track.
Second-generation ironworker Art Kelly says that when he is on the high iron,
he considers the three feet in front of his boots to be his entire world. (February 1998)

team and, later on, a new ball-park, major-league baseball might be successful in Seattle. That was the dream.

What turned the dream to reality, Isaki said, was "an improbable, wild, wonderful season in 1995 that made it okay for perhaps the first time in the history of major-league baseball in this community for people to care about baseball."

Even before the public outpouring in 1995, there were always loyal Mariners fans who cared deeply. They were the foundation on which the later broad support was built. A prime example: Sally Flood, a retired schoolteacher in her 70s and a resident of Seattle's Queen Anne Hill. She attended the first game the Mariners ever played, in 1977. A few years later, when she retired and could concentrate on the team, she bought season tickets and eventually could rattle off her section, row, and seat numbers, both at the Kingdome and at SAFECO Field, from memory: "They're just like my Social Security or Group Health numbers," she said matter-of-factly. She attended 40 or 50 games per year. "I used to go to six games in a row, but that's hard, in terms of late nights but also the emotional expenditure." She could handle four or five consecutive games nicely, however.

When the miracle season of 1995 ended, Flood was so distraught that she called her doctor. "Those were the happiest days of my life; it was the thrill of my life. But suddenly it was over and there was nothing. I couldn't

sleep—one whole night I couldn't sleep at all. But then the nurse told me the same thing had happened with her. So I took a Tylenol and felt better."

She would score all the games, of course, and listen on the radio through her earphones as the game unfolded in front of her. "I drive to games with neighbors. There are five of us on the hill who have season tickets. We buy a parking pass. It costs a couple of hundred bucks, but it's worth it [for] guaranteed parking. In years before, I would take the bus, or my daughter would pick me up, or I would ride home with somebody."

Flood caught baseball fever at age 10 or 11 when neighbors took her to Sicks' Stadium to see the Seattle Rainiers, and she later accumulated an extensive baseball

The ballpark site appears chaotic as seen from the top of the north runway. On any given day during the first year of construction piles were driven, forms built, iron erected, and concrete poured. (February 1998)

37

library. Now, "I don't like to go to bed without knowing the score. I get depressed when they lose but sleep so well when they win."

Sally Flood represents a multitude of fans—not just fans of baseball but also people who care passionately about other interests. For some it might be Chihuly's glasswork. For others it might be Wagner's *Ring Cycle*. Or motor-car racing, sailing, rock climbing, Civil War strategies, chess, birding, fine wines. Those who develop intense interests are vital in spirit; those who have sunk into anomie, listlessness, deep funk, who care deeply about nothing, are barely half alive. In this era of separation, there is intrinsic value in joining in the joy of commitment—to risk, for example, looking foolish in happy abandon as Griffey smacks another home run or A-Rod steals second base. To really care!

Battles Won, Ballpark Rises on First Avenue

Well before that improbable, wild, wonderful season of 1995 that made a multitude of Mariners fans care—really care—the club was discussing the possibility of a new ballpark.

Immediately after his election as King County executive, Gary Locke talked with club officials. Early in 1994 he appointed the King County Stadium Alternatives Task Force to study the possibility.

As part of their study, task force members invited the Mariners to provide information about the team's finances and

needs. In an unprecedented display of openness by a major-league team, Ellis responded by providing audited statements prepared by the accounting firm of Coopers & Lybrand. The statements showed mounting annual operating losses. By the end of 1994 the owners' investment had increased to $137 million.

In January 1995 the task force delivered its recommendations. Members called for a new outdoor ballpark with a retractable roof. Five months later, the Washington State Legislature passed a bill authorizing construction of a ballpark seating 45,000 people. The field was to be natural turf, covered by a retractable roof, and financed by a sales tax increase of one-tenth of 1 percent, to be collected only in King County and subject to a popular vote. The tax proceeds were earmarked first for the new park and second for repair of the damage to the Kingdome ceiling and roof caused by falling tiles in 1994. The bill also called for the Mariners to contribute $45 million toward the cost of construction.

The bill was signed into law by Governor Mike Lowry on May 22, 1995. Citizens immediately began a campaign to win public support for the stadium funding plan, which was to be voted on in King County that September. In its advocacy the campaign made two main points: a new ballpark was essential for survival of major-league baseball in Seattle, and the issue needed to be decided swiftly so the ballpark would be ready for the 1999 season.

Boom trucks pump concrete for the concourse level as ironworkers bolt up the structural steel of the north runway. (November 1998)

Darrell Bosik and Seth Bayer join other ironworkers on lunch break. For workers putting in long hours in bad weather, the half-hour breaks were a way to warm up, dry off, and rest before scaling the iron once again. (February 1998)

39

The retractable roof runs along rail systems on top of the north and south runways. The truss supporting the runways was hoisted into place by three cranes. All train traffic on this busy stretch of railroad was shut down for hours as workers raced the clock to lift the truss into place. (March 15, 1998)

BEN VANHOUTEN

From the start it was a difficult sell. The sales-tax increase was an issue with many people. The ballplayers' strike of 1994 had angered fans. Early surveys of public sentiment ran 2-to-1 against approval of the package. The campaign kicked into high gear in September; by then Griffey was back in the lineup and the Mariners were tearing up the league. Support seemed to be building daily.

In spite of the polls showing the odds against them, baseball fans by the score signed up for voluntary duty during the campaign, many before the incredible team run of September. These supporters, who under the banner of "Home Town Fans" worked the telephone lines, rallied publicly, distributed scores of pamphlets, and went door to door in many neighborhoods, mobilized a giant wave of supporters—a citizens force that ultimately played a major role in securing legislation for a new ballpark.

By election day, September 19, the election was too close to call. That night, Mariners players slipped into the clubhouse between innings to get election updates. On the field they tied their game with Texas in the ninth inning on a two-run home run by Doug Strange. In the 11th inning Griffey bounced a single to left field, knocking in the winning run. The come-from-behind victory was too late to affect the outcome of the election, but that night the measure appeared to have passed anyway, 53 percent to 47 percent.

Later that month it seemed as if every baseball fan in the United States was wearing a Mariners cap, but that night was special in Seattle. There was magic on the field, and it swept up the fans in the Kingdome and stayed with them afterward as they spilled out onto the streets, celebrated at Pioneer Square restaurants and bars, and generally savored what looked like a fairy tale come true.

Then came the absentee ballots. Slowly, over the next 10 days, the no votes caught up, then inched ahead. In the final tally, the vote was 50.1 percent against, 49.9 for.

While the absentee ballots were being counted, the Mariners drew 50,000 or more fans to the Kingdome in 10 of their next 12 games. Victories in the tiebreaker game against California, and then the classic series with the Yankees, were the best arguments anyone could make for keeping baseball in Seattle.

Presented with the election results and the pleadings of Home Town Fans, legislators and local officials expressed renewed interest in keeping the team and finding a way to build a ballpark. At the request of Governor Mike

41

Darren Pyle guides a crane operator lifting into place a two-wheeled truck assembly for the retractable roof.
These machines open and close the roof at a rate of about 30 feet per minute. (March 18, 1998)

Darren Pyle and Adam Jones check the alignment on the truck assembly. The placement of these assemblies was critical.
If the assembly was off by as little as a quarter inch either way, the next piece of the machine would not fit.

Parnelli Jones checks to make sure the assembly is plumb.

Lowry, Mariners management announced on September 29 that plans to find new owners would be postponed for another month.

While the Mariners battled Cleveland for the league championship, the state legislature approved a new financial package for building the ballpark, a measure that would include user taxes and establish a public facilities district to design and oversee construction of the field. The plan was confirmed and approved by the King County Council.

The taxes imposed were one-half of 1 percent on food and beverages sold in county restaurants, bars, and taverns; 2 percent on car rentals in King County; and a 5 percent admissions tax on events at the ballpark. The law also provided for two new baseball scratch games, to be approved by the State Lottery Commission. In addition, the state authorized King County to impose an .017 percent sales tax, which is offset against the sales tax collected by the state in King County. The result: no sales-tax increase to the public.

Soon after the first of the year, the seven members of the public facilities district—formally called the Washington State Major League Baseball Stadium Public Facilities District, but known hereafter as the PFD—were appointed. Governor Mike Lowry named three members: Joan Enticknap, whose love of baseball is boundless but who has not permitted it to interfere with her duties as an executive vice president of Seafirst Bank; Ron Judd, executive secretary of the King County Labor Council; and Charles V. (Tom) Gibbs, former executive director of Metro, later senior vice president of CH2M Hill, and like Enticknap an avid baseball fan.

Remembering his appointment, Gibbs said he'd been wondering what he wanted to do upon retirement. When he and his wife heard on the radio about the formation of the PFD, their heads snapped toward each other: both recognized instantly that it was the perfect post for him.

County Executive Locke named William Gerberding, former president of the University of Washington, who describes himself as a promiscuous fan because he has rooted for so many teams; Shelly Yapp, executive director of the Pike Place Market Preservation and Development Authority; Ruth Massinga, chief executive officer of the Casey Family Program; and Robert C. Wallace, owner of Bellevue's Wallace Properties, once chairman of the advisory board for the Kingdome, and a former board member of the Washington State Convention & Trade Center.

Among the first orders of business for the PFD was selection of the project architect. A panel named by the PFD narrowed the field to three firms, all with national reputations: NBBJ of Seattle, Hellmuth Obata Kassabaum (HOK) of St. Louis and Kansas City, and Ellerbe Becket, also of Kansas City. HOK was the early favorite. It had designed Camden Yards in Baltimore, Jacobs Field in Cleveland, and Coors Field in Denver. In addition, HOK had handled various projects for the Mariners, including the club's spring training facility at Peoria, Arizona.

But the panel chose NBBJ, which was founded in 1943 when four Seattle architects won a contract to expand the Puget Sound Navy Yard in Bremerton. Today it is the second-largest architectural firm in the country. As factors in its decision, the selection panel cited NBBJ's familiarity with local seismic factors as well as its affiliation with two other Seattle firms: Skilling Ward Magnusson Barkshire, one of the country's top structural steel consultants, and Shannon & Wilson, an environmental and geotechnical firm.

As its executive director, the PFD chose Ken Johnsen, a principal with Shiels Obletz Johnsen, a consulting firm based in Portland, Oregon. Johnsen, a native of Three Tree Point near Seattle and a graduate of Western Washington University, had supervised siting, design, and construction of Meydenbauer Center, a convention and theater facility in Bellevue. Named project manager for the PFD was Tony Puma, an independent project management consultant who had worked on the renovation of KeyArena, home of the Seattle SuperSonics. He stayed with the project through its development phase. Vic Oblas came on board as project manager when the project entered the construction phase. He is a veteran of a variety of civil works projects, including Metro's downtown bus tunnel and the West Point Treatment Facility.

For their part, early in 1996 the Mariners hired two ballpark experts to work on project management. One was John Palmer, named vice president for ballpark planning and development, who had helped build Camden Yards. The other was Brad Schrock, the lead designer of Coors Field. He started his own firm, Heinlein Schrock Architecture, in 1995.

From the outset, the PFD and the Mariners pledged to work cooperatively on the complex project. They established lines of communication, although both recognized that the PFD had responsibility for the project under state law.

The goodwill between the PFD and the Mariners helped minimize conflicts. Representatives traveled together to visit Camden Yards, Jacobs Field, and Coors Field. The favorite was Denver's Coors Field. "It had the most western feel," recalled Enticknap, first chair of the PFD.

The PFD adopted a schedule calling for completion of the project by March 1999. "The PFD had to come down running," recalled Gibbs, its second chair. The deadline "required parallel work instead of sequential. Government agencies are not accustomed to that speed."

Joined by NBBJ and the Mariners, PFD members started looking at possible sites. At first these ranged as far south as the Kent Highlands landfill. By April 1996 the PFD had narrowed the possibilities to the parking lot immediately north of the Kingdome; the parking lot immediately south of the Kingdome;

Iron beams are flown into place for the seating bowl. (July 1998)

June 1998: Work deck for roof constructed. Concrete, ironwork on grandstand seating bowl.

John "Red" Dyer works on bolting the steel trusses together. Red followed his uncles into the trade. (March 1998)

and the so-called Ackerley site, south across Royal Brougham Way from the Kingdome. On May 7, 1996, the PFD chose the Ackerley site.

By then the principals had agreed on the essential ingredients: The traditional feel of brick and steel. A natural grass field. An asymmetric playing area. Seats for about 47,000. A retractable roof.

An ironworker maneuvers steel into place on top of the seating bowl near the main entrance. (July 1998)

When PFD members saw the architect's first schematic designs, they were exuberant. The preliminary drawings looked just right.

Another of the PFD's essential tasks in the first months of operation was selection of a general contractor. After a careful process, the PFD selected the joint project team of Huber Hunt & Nichols—a firm with a national reputation for ballpark work—and Kiewit Construction Company of Seattle. Huber Hunt was the general contractor for Bank One Ballpark in Phoenix.

An environmental impact statement was approved in September, and the task began of acquiring property from private owners of parcels on the site. Some businesses had been in the same location for decades. Not until the early months of 1997 was the final settlement reached.

During this period the Mariners and the PFD had negotiated and reached a development agreement, but they had not negotiated a long-term lease for occupancy. Significant issues remained. These included the amount of rent to be paid by the Mariners, establishment of capital reserves, profit sharing, and responsibility for operation of the ballpark.

Negotiations slouched into December 1996. That month the PFD threatened to announce a delay in the start of the project unless an agreement was reached on the lease. On December 12 the team received a letter from four members of the King County

Council that to the Mariners sounded threatening.

Would construction be delayed? To the Mariners, it seemed so. From the start, club officials had declared that they would not sustain financial losses beyond the 1998 season. Without assurances of a new field in time for the 1999 season, it was clear to the Mariners' owners that they had no remaining alternative but to put the team up for sale.

And so on December 14, at a televised news conference, Ellis announced that the owners had decided to discontinue discussions about a new park and would offer the team for sale immediately. "It was not a bluff," Ellis recalled later. "It was a very bad day, one of the worst days of my career."

The announcement caused wide consternation. The dream of a first-rate field was disappearing, and it seemed likely the team would disappear too. Then, into the breach rode Senator Slade Gorton. Again.

It was not the first time Gorton had helped major-league baseball stay in Seattle. He played an important role in forcing major-league baseball to return to Seattle after the Pilots left in 1969. That

A security guard is dwarfed by
the first completed truss of the
roof. At the top of the arch,
the truss is 220 feet above
the ground. (July 1998)

July 1998: First truss of roof completed.
Iron for sun canopy installed.

PUBLIC FACILITIES DISTRICT

was Gorton's first rescue. The second came when Jeff Smulyan offered the Mariners for sale in 1991, and Gorton made contact with Nintendo interests.

Ellis is Gorton's oldest Seattle friend. They first met at a Young Republicans meeting in 1956, shortly after Gorton had arrived in Seattle to begin practicing law. In December 1996 Gorton was vacationing with his family in Hawaii during the week that Ellis announced the team was going to be sold. "I stepped off the plane that Saturday night when we got home and reporters asked me what I thought about sale of the Mariners. All I could say was 'Huh?'"

So he called Ellis that evening with his offer to help. The next day, Sunday, Gorton started working with the county council and the PFD. Late that week, after conferring with Ellis, Gorton and others wrote up the conditions under which the Mariners would stay in Seattle.

"It seemed reasonable. And on Friday, at a big news conference, I announced the conditions. The county and PFD accepted immediately. The city wouldn't go along. Ellis made some further minor concessions. And the deal was done."

It sounds simple now, but at the time it was a cliff-hanger whose ending was entirely uncertain. On January 13, after various concessions that made possible a timely start of construction, the Mariners withdrew the plan to sell the team.

At last the idea of a ballpark became reality. On March 8, the PFD and the Mariners sponsored a groundbreaking celebration, and Seattle witnessed another outpouring of fan interest and loyalty. Attendance was astonishing. Police estimated those on hand at 15,000. But announcer Dave Niehaus, well experienced in estimating the size of crowds, put the figure at 30,000. One who came very early was a 90-year-old woman who wanted to be first in line.

Many came with shovels, spades, trowels, even plastic spoons—it was, after all, a groundbreaking—and hacked away at the hard earth where the grandstands would soon rise. Ken Griffey Jr., who flew to Seattle from spring training in Arizona, joked that his excavation tool was a backhoe parked nearby. One writer called it wacky but wonderful, "marked by exaggeration, sentiment, and fireworks." Those present sang "Take Me Out to the Ball Game," and kids ran bases set up on a quickly improvised diamond.

Bill and Anita Lyons of Kent brought their grandchildren, Tyler, 6, and Nicole Arrington, 7. "We're all Mariners nuts here," said Bill Lyons proudly. "We stuck with them through thick and thin. We worked with them to get out the votes and now we just want to see all the animosity go away. We just want everyone to be together and have some baseball." The turnout thrilled members of the PFD. "People put rancor aside," the PFD's Enticknap recalled. "It was a reaffirmation of feeling for baseball."

Loose ends remained. A

49

Paul Isaki shows Jay Buhner the progress on the ballpark.

Jay Buhner talks with ironworker Art Kelly.

The ballpark is reflected in Jay Buhner's glasses during a tour. (July 1998)

group called Citizens for More Important Things circulated petitions calling for a vote on the issuance of bonds and claimed it had collected more than 70,000 signatures. But on February 26, 1997, Judge Kathleen Learned of King County Superior Court ruled the initiative invalid. The ruling was immediately appealed to the state supreme court. PFD attorneys asked for an expedited decision, but the higher court did not rule until Friday, June 13. By a 7-2 vote, the lower court decision was upheld.

While insiders were working to set up the mechanics that would permit construction of the ballpark, baseball fans stayed focused on the team.

During much of the 1996 summer, injuries to the two best Mariners players hindered the team's race for another title in the American League West. A pitch broke a bone in Ken Griffey Jr.'s right hand and he was out from June 20 to July 14, when he returned to the lineup with a homer and a double, driving in three runs.

Even more serious was Randy Johnson's aching back, which nearly wiped out his 1996 season. He was on the disabled list for much of the season, pitching only 61 innings, although his record was 5-0 and his earned run average was 3.67. An operation on a

Edgar Martinez walks onto the field for a ceremonial batting practice. (July 1998)

Ken Griffey Jr. signs balls for workers at the topping-out festivities. (July 1998)

Carrying on a long-standing tradition, workers sign the last beam before it is hoisted into place during the topping-out ceremony.
"Topping out" means the basic structure is complete; the work then moves into the finishing stages. (July 1998)

herniated disc in his lower back was performed in September.

Russ Davis, the third baseman, broke his foot and was lost for the season. A collision with catcher John Marzano put Edgar Martinez on the sidelines for 21 games. Outfielder Jay Buhner also lost a week to an ankle injury.

But there was good news, too.

Five Mariners, a record number, were named to the American League All-Star team: Griffey, of course, although he was injured and could not play in the game, plus Alex Rodriguez, Dan Wilson, Martinez, and Buhner.

Rodriguez, barely more than a rookie, had an extraordinary year, leading the league in average at

.358. Griffey hit 49 home runs and Buhner smacked 40, also winning his first Gold Glove Award.

Again the Mariners added to their roster for the stretch drive, acquiring pitchers Jamie Moyer and Terry Mulholland, plus outfielder Mark Whiten and infielder Dave Hollins. The

Mariners pulled to within one game of the lead with a week to go. But Texas won the West by 4½ games. Still, the Mariners drew a record 2,723,850 at home and were a hot draw on the road. About this time the *New York Times* declared that the Mariners were probably baseball's most glamorous team.

Ken Griffey Jr. signs a shirt for a worker.   *As a harbinger of things to come, Ken Griffey Jr. knocks a ball into the park. (July 1998)*

51

Challenges: Wind, Rain, Water, Soil, History

In June 1997, work on the park began at last. By then the PFD had gained ownership of the site. The first step was demolition of the buildings that had to be cleared before construction could begin.

The area south of Pioneer Square had once been tidelands, including 3,000 acres of mudflats. Early in Seattle's history, knocking down the city's steep hills was a civic passion. The earth from nearby cuts (around Dearborn Street and Yesler Way) and from the Denny Regrade (which leveled a hill just north of downtown) was sluiced onto Elliott Bay's shoreline, eventually filling 1,400 acres. In *King County and Its Queen City: Seattle*, James R. Warren wrote of the period after 1900: "An important Seattle industrial and commercial area developed on those former mud-flats. Sears, Roebuck and Company's regional headquarters is located there, as are several foundries, a brewery, the railroad marshaling yards, military ship-ping areas, and many other indus-tries." And now a ballpark.

But to truly understand the site upon which SAFECO Field stands, it's necessary to go back further—about 15,000 years, as a matter of fact. At that time Puget Sound and Seattle were covered by a sheet of ice 3,000 feet thick. This massive glacier reached south from the Fraser River in what is now British Columbia to just south of Olympia and west almost to Shelton.

"Great loads of glacially bull-dozed rock, gravel, and finer materials were dumped or washed into irregular beds, piles, mounds, and hilly stripes to cover the underlying bedrock," wrote Arthur R. Kruckeberg in his book *The Natural History of Puget Sound Country*. "The present pat-terning of the land is thus trace-able to ice-age events of the recent past, reaching a climax about 18,000 to 13,000 years ago."

Puget Sound has been covered by ice many times; the ice sheet described by Kruckeberg was only the most recent. If there had been humans around the Sound at the time, no doubt they would have been pleased that this particular ice age lasted no more than 1,500 years. By 11,000 years ago the glacier had receded to the Canadian border, leaving behind such spectacular waterways as Lake Sammamish, Lake Washington, Puget Sound, and Hood Canal.

When historian Will Durant remarked that "civilization exists by geological consent—subject to change without notice," he must have been thinking of the Pacific Northwest. Just off the Northwest coast, the Juan de Fuca tectonic plate drives under the continental North American plate to its east, at the rate of three or four cen-timeters per year. The convergence of the two plates becomes the stage on which seismic activity takes place. In modern-day Seattle, that has led to an earth-quake in 1949 that measured 7.1 (major) on the Richter scale, as well as a tremor in 1965 of magnitude 6.5 (large).

Jason Volk, left, and Brian Jones guide the last beam into place, marking completion of the structure of the ballpark. (July 29, 1998)

With hoots and hollers from the workers below, Brian Jones stands atop the last beam and salutes his colleagues. (July 29, 1998)

Elvis Childs bolts steel beams together for the sun canopy on First Avenue. (June 1998)

The field and downtown Seattle are framed by a door on the upper-level seating area. (July 1998)

Like dancers in a choreographed ballet, ironworkers push and pull a leg of the roof as a crane lifts it off the ground. (June 1998)

Workers hang iron at the ballpark. Ironworkers are the cowboys of construction sites—independent, proud, and seemingly fearless as they walk narrow beams hundreds of feet above the ground. (June 1998)

Thus the new ballpark's architects and designers faced two problems. First, Seattle sits on a major earthquake fault that periodically rumbles with powerful tremors. Second, a severe quake can turn the loose soil of a landfill into mush—a process called liquefaction. It magnifies the power of the temblor and imposes extraordinary stress on structures. Much of Seattle's waterfront is landfill.

The city's seismic proclivity and the site's landfill added millions of dollars to construction costs. But all construction on the fill of south Seattle faces the same problems, and there are solutions. The sheet of ice that covered Seattle a few years ago, for instance, did more than just churn up the mixture of sand, gravel, and rocks called glacial till. As it receded, the weight of the ice packed the glacial till so compactly that today it is sometimes called soft rock. By driving piles through the fill and into the till, a solid foundation can be built.

The bearing soil under SAFECO Field slopes from north to south, 75 to 120 feet under the fill. A total of 1,450 steel pilings were driven into the solid soil to support the grandstands, according to Ralph Belton, technical designer for NBBJ, and 280 support the garage. The pilings slid easily through the landfill, he said, but when they reached and penetrated the underlying till, it was almost like hitting rock. The pilings are tied together and stabilized at their top by concrete caps; as a result, if all the landfill were cleared away, the grandstands would remain, a safe island perched on stilts.

Before Seattle started turning its mountains into molehills by dumping them on the waterfront, the tideflats were crisscrossed by railroad trestles that carried trains taking cargo to ships in Elliott Bay. Remnants of the trestles were uncovered as the field was excavated.

The image of the trestles pleased Rick Zieve, NBBJ's lead designer, because it is subtly repeated on the roof of the ballpark. "What we've essentially ended up with is two steel trestles on either side [of the retractable roof] that support the tracks. That hearkens back to the turn-of-the-century kind of views of Pioneer Square and that area, where the railroads were all built up on trestles going across this exact site."

Another challenge facing construction workers was that the water table is only a half-dozen feet or so below surface level. "It's like excavating a bathtub," remarked Palmer of the Mariners.

The high water table profoundly affected the design of the park. It meant the playing field could not be lower than street level, unlike Camden Yards and Coors Field. Designers turned this sour apple into sweet cider by building a dramatic stairway via which spectators enter the park and climb to the grand concourse. By coincidence, the dimensions of the rotunda at the entrance are exactly the same as that of the old Ebbets Field in Brooklyn.

A. Bartlett Giamatti, the former president of Yale University who became baseball commissioner for a brief period before a heart

attack took his life, wrote about the importance of a ballpark's entrance in his book *Take Time for Paradise*:

"When we enter that simulacrum of a city, the arena or stadium or ballpark, and we have successfully, usually in a crowd, negotiated the thoroughfares of this special, set-aside city, past the portals, guarded by those who check our fitness and take the special token of admission, past the sellers of food, the vendors of programs, who make their markets and cry their news, and after we ascend the ramp or go through the tunnel and enter the inner core of the little city, we often are struck, at least I am, by the suddenness and fullness of the vision

August 1998: Second roof truss completed. Sun canopy roofing installed. Structure for scoreboard, bleacher seats installed.

PUBLIC FACILITIES DISTRICT

Fog obscures the scoreboard structure as ironworkers walk across the steel. (August 1998)

there presented: a green expanse, complete and coherent, shimmering, carefully tended, a garden…"

In simpler words, Giamatti enjoyed stepping into a ballpark and catching that first glimpse of the playing field. The late colum-

nist Red Smith also commented upon the metaphysical beauty of the baseball field:

"Ninety feet between the bases represents man's closest approach to absolute truth. The world's fastest man cannot run to first base

ahead of a sharply hit ball that is cleanly handled by an infielder; he will get there only half a step too late. Let the fielder juggle the ball for one moment or delay his throw an instant and the runner will be safe. Ninety feet demands perfec-

tion. It accurately measures the cunning, speed and finesse of the base stealer against the velocity of a thrown ball. It dictates the placement of infielders. That single dimension makes baseball a fine art—and nobody knows for sure how it came to be."

Before the beauty of SAFECO Field could be realized, however, its architects had to deal with the hard practicalities. They at first presumed the water under the field was tidal and would be saline or at least brackish. But the water level does not seem to fluctuate with the tides; upon testing, the water was found to be fresh, probably runoff from nearby Beacon Hill or maybe from the Duwamish River system. A system was developed that used the underground water to irrigate the field. A network of underground pipes collects the water, and a series of pumps sends the overflow into the storm sewers. Some water is collected in a holding tank and then is pumped back into the irrigation system.

Yet another element considered by designers was the wind. A study of historical weather patterns showed that during Seattle's rainy periods, the wind usually comes from the southwest. But during the summer, when most baseball games are played, the wind in Seattle comes from the

September 1998:
First section of retractable roof installed.

PUBLIC FACILITIES DISTRICT

north. Designers concluded from weather studies that they should put the highest wall of the park on Atlantic Street, where it would provide shelter from south winds during rainy seasons. In effect, the park is turning its back to the wet weather, just as Northwesterners hunch their shoulders and turn their backs to the rain during windy rainstorms. But the lower end of the grandstands along Royal Brougham Way will be open to the dry north winds of summer.

Fortunately, that orientation coincided with the preference of Major League Baseball for putting the third-base line five degrees on either side of true north. Palmer remembered, "People said, 'Why didn't you just turn it and put home plate back by the railroad, out here in the southeast corner, so the whole ballpark would look out at the Sound and the Olympics?' Well, if we had done that, our batters would just be staring into the setting sun.

"There are some parks that have an orientation of north right up the middle [from catcher

The first roof truss took over a month to complete, as shown in these photographs taken on June 8, June 23, and July 6, 1998. The rest of the trusses were completed in an average of 14 days.

Too large to capture even with an extreme-wide-angle lens, the first roof section is shown in four photographs, from south to north. (September 1998)

The cable that will hold the "eyebrow" section of the roof is delivered. (September 1998)

through second base to center field], which turns it a little more, and that has been approved by the league. We preferred to stay a little closer to our orientation of the third base to north, and that essentially pushed the home-plate corner down to the southwest.

"Right field will essentially be our sun field," Palmer said. "If you come out here at 5:30 for batting practice, that whole right-field grandstand will just be bathed in the sun."

Once the orientation of the field was settled, NBBJ arranged for wind-tunnel tests with RWDI, a firm near Toronto. The wind analysis dealt in part with how the wind would affect the roof, and how big the motors that move it would need to be.

The wind analysis also led to relocation of the big scoreboard, which is now in center field, noted Belton of NBBJ; in its earlier location in left field, it had created a wind swirl. "We also did some things in the back of the roof, and once we did that the swirls stopped. Now we basically have a fairly neutral ballpark relative to the wind, even when the wind is blowing up to 20 to 30 miles an hour. And that's important, because when you get the swirls it

October 1998: First roof section rolled over ballpark. Eyebrow hung. Lights installed.

PUBLIC FACILITIES DISTRICT

starts to get unpredictable."

In Seattle there are rare summer days when, despite a north wind, it rains. When that happens, moisture may blow under the roof and onto the outfield grandstands. By one estimate, however, this will happen only once in three years. The roof

Tied off with rock-climbing gear, workers put insulation and roofing material on the eyebrow section of the roof. (February 1999)

With the main part of the roof completed, ironworkers and painters work on the east eyebrow. (May 1999)

An ironworker's shadow hits the concrete of the temporary structure supporting the work platform for the roof. (March 1999)

Under the shadow of an unfinished roof truss, a worker caulks an opening in the east wall of the ballpark. (September 1998)

offers cover, not enclosure.

Just how the cold, dank air of Puget Sound would affect the flight of the baseball was unknown at first. The wind-tunnel studies and simple physics calculations gave some ideas, however. For instance, a home run hit in the Kingdome by Mark McGwire several years ago, when he was still in the American League at

Workers relay materials up a scaffolding behind the scoreboard structure. (December 16, 1998)

Oakland, would have cleared SAFECO Field's fences and the left-field wall and landed somewhere on Royal Brougham Way. Because of the heavy air, SAFECO Field's fences are 20 or 30 feet shorter than those of Coors Field. Baseballs don't fly as far in Seattle as in mile-high Denver, where the air is thinner.

The exact distances to SAFECO Field's fences were being adjusted quite late in the ballpark's construction. Historically, the Mariners have relied heavily on long-ball hitting, so it was to be expected that flexibility in distances to the fences would be retained in some areas of the park. Will Griffey hit 56 homers at his previous years' pace? Stay tuned.

Manager Piniella agreed that the Mariners "have hit the home-run ball for the years I've been here. The Kingdome is homer friendly—it's indoors, it's climate controlled, and if you get the ball up in the air, it will go. But when you go outdoors, no matter how you plan, you don't know how the ball will carry, not until you get there.

"Weather has a lot to do with it. Indoors it has no effect at all. When I played in Seattle back in the late '60s at old Sicks' Stadium [he played three years for Portland in the PCL when Seattle was still in that league], the ball didn't carry at all to left field, but it did carry to right. When it was damp and cold, it didn't carry at all. So it remains to be seen how it will go."

A gull enjoys the view from the top of the entry. (December 1998)

Scaffolding is set up for bricklayers at the main entrance of the ballpark. (October 1998)

Workers Bring Bravado, Commitment to Job

Construction began in June 1997 with "two concurrent operations almost simultaneously," Palmer recalls. "One was the driving of piles. . . . So on the most southern [parking] lot of the Kingdome, down in the southeast corner, we started driving in piles."

At the same time demolition crews, working counterclockwise, started at the corner of Royal Brougham Way and First Avenue, diagonally across the field from the pile-driving operation. By the time demolition had been completed south to Atlantic, pile driving, which was proceeding clockwise, had reached the same intersection. With the buildings cleared away, pile driving continued north along First Avenue. It was then time to let contracts for foundations, grading, pile caps,

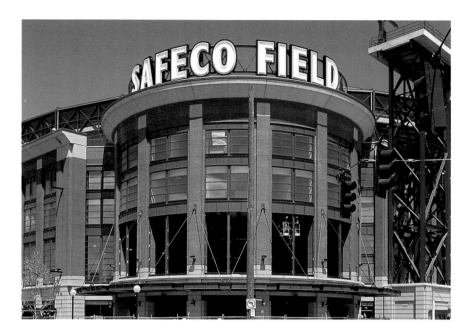

The rotunda welcoming fans to the ballpark nears completion. (June 1999)

The brick and concrete details of the main entrance are reminiscent of some of the older structures in the area. (December 1998)

and concrete work.

The concrete caps atop the piles were crisscrossed with steel rebar that tied tightly into the concrete slabs at grade level, fixing the piles firmly in place, at the bottom anchored in soft stone and at the top capped in concrete and steel reinforcing.

Dealing with the possibility of earthquakes was the biggest challenge facing the ballpark's designers. They responded by creating a building that, in an earthquake, will sway rather than crumble. Six expansion joints, which divide the ballpark into six independent structures, allow the ballpark to rock without self-destructing. The joints are one inch wide on the Main Concourse and six inches wide on the upper.

Two other imaginative features designed to prevent serious seismic damage are built into the roof. On the Royal Brougham side, the roof is hinged on large pins where trusses support the

65

roof. If the roof should start to rock during a tremor, the hinges will provide flexibility to prevent the motion from being conveyed into the trusses. In the roof near the pins are giant shock absorbers that will transform the quake's energy into harmless heat. Hydraulic cylinders filled with oil, they resemble automobile shock absorbers except that they're about 14 feet long.

Once the piles were sunk, fastened securely at top and bottom, capped with slabs of concrete six feet deep, interlaced with rebar, and connected with grade beams, other work started.

With the extensive foundation laid, the big push was to pour concrete for the Main Concourse. Once that was accomplished, steel construction began, an equally complex operation. Roughly 20,000 tons of steel went into SAFECO Field: 11 tons in the grandstands and 9 tons in the roof. Piece by piece, the steel was delivered in the order it would be erected. A long cable raised six or eight pieces of steel high in the air. Ironworkers swung each piece into position and fastened it with bolts.

All this took large numbers of workers, the unsung heroes in the construction of SAFECO Field. Noting the large number of local firms that won contracts, the PFD's Johnsen commented, "It's cost effective when work is done by a local firm. Also, they enjoy being involved in a local project. The workers take pride in it. We got good workmanship because of their pride. At times there were about 850 people who got up and

went to work every morning on the ballpark and were proud of it." Twenty-five percent of the work force were women or minorities, and almost 15 percent were apprentices. Later in construction, when plumbers, electricians, and finishers were on the site, employment expanded to 1,400 to 1,500 workers.

They worked during the pleasant, sunny days of summer but also during the wet, nasty days of winter, carrying out their tasks with impressive speed and efficiency. Many emblazoned Mariners mottos, such as "You gotta love these guys," on their safety helmets. A number had worked on the renovation of KeyArena, home court of the Sonics, and after finishing SAFECO Field crossed Royal Brougham Way to work on the Seahawks' new football stadium. "That will be a threepeat," carpenter Dan Slate of Everett said. "Work on the ballpark is more difficult than the usual job, different from a square building." His comments were echoed by others, who seemed to relish the departure from typical construction work—in part because many were Mariners fans.

Some of the carpenters, such as Greg Child of Carnation and Ken Schorno of Mount Vernon, have been colleagues for a long time. "I've worked with Greg for six years," said Schorno, who played Little League baseball and later softball. He worked on KeyArena and is a fan of the Sonics as well as the Mariners. "These are historical monuments," he said. "I'll tell my kids about it. They'll say,

Surveyor Christine McClain enjoys the sun during a lunch break at the ballpark. She says she is proud to be involved in a project like this one. (December 1997)

Flagger Irma Harris watches traffic while waiting for the next big truck to come on site. (September 1998)

A man takes advantage of the late-afternoon sun to inspect the seating-area concrete. (December 1998)

67

Hanging out over the leg of a roof section, painter Ed Sipes stretches to reach a difficult spot. (March 1999)

Kevin Wilson spray-paints steel beams that will tie together the larger beams of the roof. (September 1998)

Attending to detail work that all homeowners can relate to, Richard Hoo paints the crevices of the first roof span. (July 6, 1998)

'My dad worked on that.'" Child, a foreman, spoke with pride about working on the grand staircase: "It's the first thing people will see."

Kim Doeleman of SeaTac started work at SAFECO Field in May 1998 as a plumber's apprentice. She proudly displayed Jay Buhner's autograph on her safety helmet, collected during his visit to the park that summer. She became a plumber after attending a pre-apprenticeship program for women, having become handy with tools while growing up because her mother relied on her to fix things, including cars.

Beth Wilson of Seattle and Adrian Gates of Bothell worked at SAFECO Field as journeyman plumbers. Both expressed pride in their contributions to the ballpark, agreeing that they'll enjoy telling their kids about working on it. They're pleased that their high-quality work will benefit the public for years to come.

Laborer Ron Vincent of Marysville was an outstanding

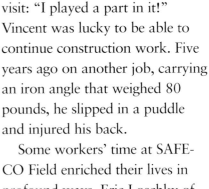

football and baseball player at Wenatchee Valley Junior College. He spoke of his pride in working on a landmark that many will visit: "I played a part in it!" Vincent was lucky to be able to continue construction work. Five years ago on another job, carrying an iron angle that weighed 80 pounds, he slipped in a puddle and injured his back.

Some workers' time at SAFECO Field enriched their lives in profound ways. Eric Loschky of Seattle was one of those who progressed from apprentice to journeyman status while working at SAFECO Field, thereby enhancing the local pool of skilled workers. The progression enabled him to buy a house and get married. While Jeff Kerby of Boise worked at SAFECO Field, he helped both his wife and daughter study at Boise State College. "Big jobs like this help pay for it," he said. He became a Mariners fan after starting work at SAFECO Field.

The kings of the hill were the ironworkers, who walked beams hundreds of feet in the air with seeming nonchalance while the roof was being built. They were a cocky bunch, joking and joshing while putting away immense lunches. One of them, Art Kelly, talked about the need to concentrate while walking on the roof. "Don't look around," he advised. "The few feet in front of you are the whole world." Only half kidding, Art Kelly asserted that the ironworkers are the stars of the construction world; perhaps not surprisingly, his co-workers John (Red) Dyer, Dan Youso, Bret Miller, and Darren Pyle agreed.

Ironworker Michael Tom, known by his initials of MT, enthused about how the Mariners gave each person on his work crew a ticket to a game with Cleveland in 1998. Mariners players also visited the workers at the construction site and seemed impressed with the energy and skill the workers brought to the job.

While work was under way on the grandstand, construction progressed simultaneously on the roof. That was a neater trick than it might seem. Space over the railroad tracks on the eastern edge of the park was leased from Burlington Northern. Next to the tracks was established an on-site manufacturing site—a mini-facto-

A likeness of the Seattle Rainiers' famous pitcher Fred Hutchinson is embossed on the endpiece of each row of seats. (October 1998)

Carpenter Matthew Reis epoxies seat anchors in the bowl.

ry, really—where the roof could be fabricated without interfering with grandstand construction. The ability to work simultaneously on the grandstand and the roof eliminated scheduling and staging conflicts. Availability of the space was important after completion of the ballpark, too; it's where the three panels of the roof are stacked when open.

The Erection Company of Redmond put up a working platform 200 feet in the air, called the "dance floor," from which the roof panels were constructed. Three shoring towers, or hydraulic jacks, bore the weight as the ironworkers put together the 1,000-ton trusses.

Panels 1 and 3 were construct-ed first. Then the dance floor was elevated by 45 feet and Panel 2 was put together. Panels 1 and 3 nest under Panel 2 when retract-ed, reducing the storage space necessary.

When bids were advertised for design and construction of the roof, a leading contender for the contract was Mitsubishi Heavy Industries. Mitsubishi was on the original team of NBBJ, the archi-tects, but bidding rules required a competition. Two other firms joined Mitsubishi in the competi-tion: AeroGo, an offshoot of Boeing that builds air and water casters, and Ederer of Seattle.

Ederer won the competition and joined NBBJ as a Seattle firm entrusted with a vital role in con-

February 1999: Field excavated. Seats installed. One section of roof rolled to west. Brick installed on facade.

71

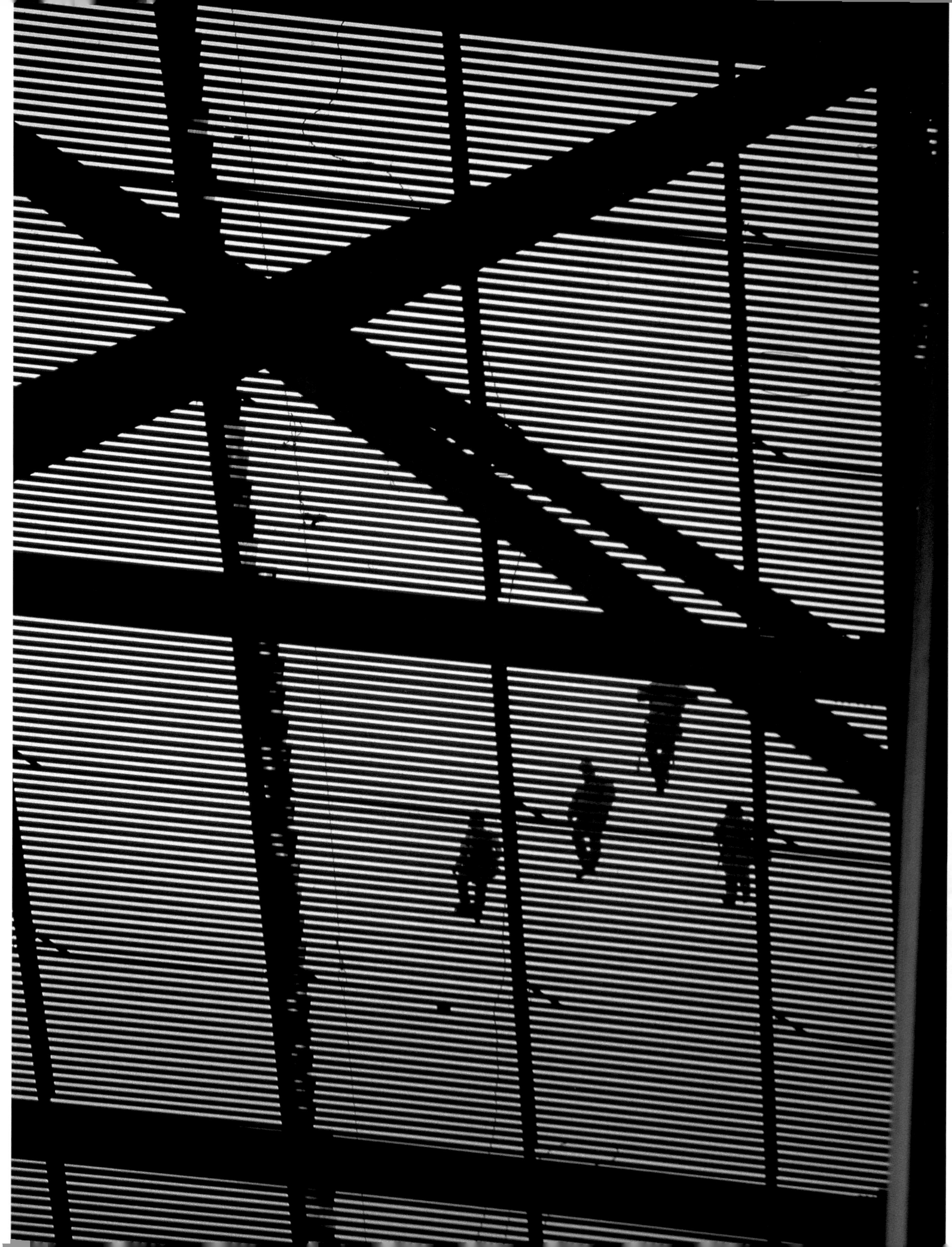

With the first roof section completed and rolled out of the way, ironworkers construct the next sections. In the grandstand, workers install seats and begin to lower the field to its final level. (November 1998)

Photographed from below the decking, ironworkers become silhouettes as they walk on the roof. (December 1998)

struction of SAFECO Field, adding more homegrown flavor to the project. "We were introduced to the ballpark and retractable roof the same way citizens were," recalled Ederer president Neil Skogland, "by reading about it in the newspapers."

Ederer is one of those Seattle companies that are largely anonymous locally but have a wide international reputation. Established in 1901, it's hidden in the industrial section of south Seattle, a short walk down First Avenue from SAFECO Field. But its cranes are all over the Seattle and Tacoma waterfronts and in other ports, too, around the globe. And it built a 325-ton crane for the National Aeronautics and Space Administration at Cape Kennedy, probably the firm's most technical job, as well as two cranes that lift the space shuttles to the lift pads from the vehicle assembly building at Kennedy.

Ederer's cranes are used to lift everything from radioactive waste to molten metal to rocket motors.

Selection of Ederer "was a great break for the park," declared Gibbs, chair of the PFD. To Zieve of NBBJ, the most fascinating thing about Ederer was that "this company that none of us knew about" was located so close to the site—a mere 20 blocks away, as it turned out.

The retraction mechanism for moving the three panels of the roof is almost identical to that used for the variety of big cranes Ederer has been building for years. It consists of 128 steel wheels that look like railroad wheels arranged in groups of eight. These 16 wheeled assemblies run along elevated runways on the lip of the stadium. The lower height and open legs permit a view north, over the outfield, of Seattle's skyscrapers, Elliott Bay, and, in the distance, the Olympic

Mountains.

The power for the 36-inch wheels comes from 96 ten-horse-power DC motors. The roof is designed to move at about 30 feet per minute, a very slow walking pace, normally taking 20 minutes to open or close. If necessary, however, the speed can be increased to 60 feet per minute. Two of the roof panels are 631 feet long; the third is 655 feet. By comparison, the center span of Seattle's Aurora Bridge is 800 feet. The roof covers 8.9 acres. The lowest truss is 167 feet above field level; however, the trusses are in foul territory over the stands. The total weight of the roof is given variously as 11,000 tons and 13,000 tons. The whole ballpark contains enough structural steel to build a 60-story high-rise: 250 tons, measuring 270 miles, plus 62,000 cubic yards of concrete.

The position of the panels can be controlled to within a fraction

73

of an inch. When the roof is opened or closed, five people make sure that switches are aligned and that there's no debris on the rails. Eight runway-mounted cameras give operators clear views of the tracks. Movement is controlled electronically.

The roof is designed to withstand the weight of six or seven feet of snow and winds up to 70 miles per hour. In peak storms it will shed 9,500 gallons of water per minute—the equivalent of 500 bathtubs emptying per minute, or 2,000 toilets flushing per minute, or 1,000 hoses emptying per minute.

Enter now another Seattle firm with an international reputation: Skilling Ward Magnusson Barkshire, consulting structural and civil engineers, founded in 1923. Its structures have been erected in 36 states and 27 countries.

Jon Magnusson, chairman and chief executive officer of Skilling, holds degrees in engineering from the University of Washington and the University of California at Berkeley. He's been principal-in-charge of many of Skilling's biggest sports projects. Zieve of NBBJ gives Magnusson credit for the turned-down legs that support the roof. This unremarkable-sounding feature was a key to the openness of the park and "the biggest innovation that came out of this roof," according to Zieve.

The turned-down legs connect to the trusses on which rest the wheels and rails, built by Ederer, that open and close the roof. The legs were a key to providing a visual connection to the city's vistas. The relative simplicity of design, also credited to Skilling, ensured that the roof was reliable and efficient.

Eight shock absorbers are mounted in the trusses at the north end of the roof panels. Automobile shock absorbers are two inches in diameter and designed for forces from 1,000 to 2,000 pounds. The dampers in the retractable roof are 14 feet long, 18 inches in diameter, and designed to withstand forces up to 1.6 million pounds. They effectively cut in half the maximum seismic forces imposed on the roof, runway, and travel-truck system.

Almost everyone agrees that baseball is best when played outside. So why, then, was a retractable roof so important? Ellis explained that the main purpose of the roof is to guarantee "to somebody coming from out of town that there would be a game, but more importantly to ensure that when you were there, you would be comfortable."

Seattle can be chilly at night in April or late September. Will fans stay at home on colder evenings?

"We thought hard about whether we should seal the park and heat it," Ellis responded. "And we decided that it was an outdoor experience, that our temperature here was not that cold at any time during that period. It can get clammy in the evening. But if we could cover it during those periods, people would be perfectly happy to come in their jackets. And they would have the outdoor experience."

Ironworker Art Kelly tells a joke to John "Red" Dyer as they relax in the elevator taking them to the roof. (December 1998)

With Seattle sparkling in the background, ironworker Sonny Winston puts down decking on a section of the roof. (February 1999)

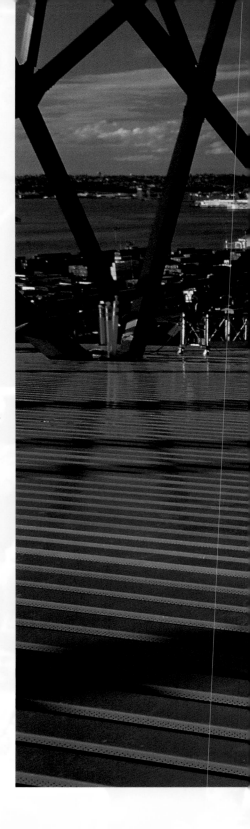

April 1999: Field leveled. Diamond laid out. Final roof truss hung.

Workers admire the view of the Olympic Mountains, Elliott Bay, and downtown Seattle from the top of the roof. (March 1999)

Beautiful Green Grass Takes Care, Passion

An integral part of the outdoor experience, of course, is a field of natural grass. Such a field was assumed from the start in the park's enabling legislation. Like Camden Yards, the new park was to feature sky and grass.

Artificial turf first appeared at the Astrodome in Houston in 1966, making domed parks feasible. Purists always disliked it, and players made nasty cracks about it. "If a horse can't eat it," quipped Dick Allen, an infielder-outfielder, "I don't want to play on it." The late Mark Belanger, a shortstop for Baltimore, remarked that artificial turf "makes good fielders into great ones, and turns poor fielders into good fielders,

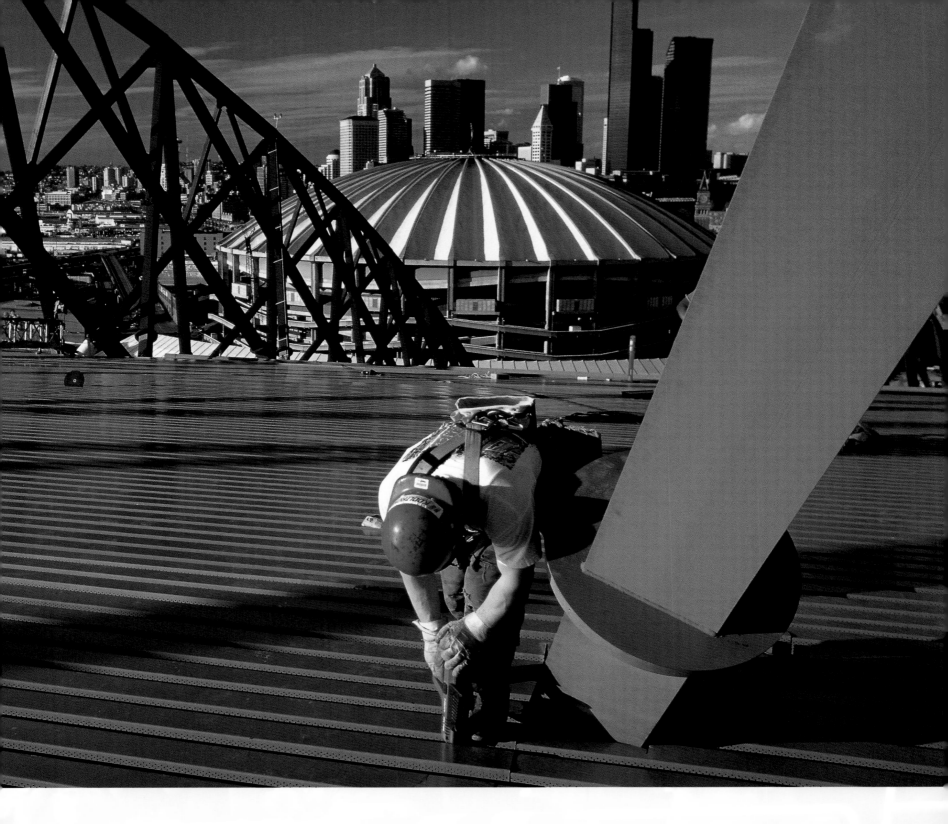

but it takes away part of the game." In the American League, only Minnesota, Toronto, and Tampa Bay still play on artificial turf; in the National League, Pittsburgh, Philadelphia, Cincinnati, Montreal, and Houston play on artificial turf.

Mariners players will definitely benefit from playing on grass at home, according to Piniella. "Grass is easier on every player, including pitchers," he observed. "The Kingdome, with AstroTurf, was very demanding on players' knees, ankles, the wear and tear,

soreness to the lower back. That'll be alleviated. At the same time, the new park will give pitchers a chance to get away from the Kingdome, where the AstroTurf is very quick and the ball also carries well. . . . And Seattle summers are so beautiful, it's a shame to

waste them indoors."

To get the turf they wanted, the Mariners turned to Roger Bossard as a consultant in designing and building the field; choosing the sand, clay, and subsurfaces of the field; doing sun-shade studies; and selecting just the

An ironworker welds bolts on part of the roof. (January 1999)

right mix of grass.

Bossard is baseball's top groundskeeper because he knows more about baseball fields than anyone else. He holds an agronomy degree from Purdue and, like his father and grandfather, is compulsive in caring for the fields under his charge. In person he's animated, friendly, and personable.

Three generations of Bossards have more than 235 collective years of experience in groundskeeping. Their fields have included Municipal Stadium in Cleveland, Sportsman's Park in St. Louis, the Polo Grounds in New York, Fenway Park in Boston, Jack Murphy Stadium in San Diego, both the old and new Comiskey Parks in Chicago, the infields at Yankee Stadium and at Pro Player Stadium in Miami, the entire field at Busch Stadium in St. Louis, and soil and grass at the new fields being built in Detroit and Milwaukee.

Bossard worked with Dr. Hank Wilkinson, a University of Illinois plant pathologist, for more than a year to find just the right strain of grass for SAFECO Field—a blend of 80 percent Kentucky bluegrass and 20 percent perennial ryegrass. "Here in Washington, people

thought bluegrass wouldn't grow
well," Bossard noted. "Truth is,
it's a prolific grower—but requires
high maintenance. It requires a lot
of things that homeowners can't
do." One of the virtues of bluegrass is that its darker, wider
blade sheds water four times
faster than rye does.

A concrete finisher stains the floor of the Rotunda to represent waves crashing to shore. (April 1999)

Workers inspect the lights above the grandstand. Each one was aimed to ensure even lighting across the field. (May 1999)

A worker on top of the roof is silhouetted against the sky. (April 1999)

As groundskeepers work on the newly installed field, the roof sections are tested. (May 1999)

Terry Butler directs a crane operator flying in a letter for SAFECO Field. (April 1999)

The first direct step in building the playing surface was taken in October 1998 when 540 truck-loads of dirt were excavated, lowering the level of the field by seven feet. The next January, four-inch drainage pipe, 7,000 feet of it, was laid. Then came 2,000 tons of pea gravel, four inches deep, in which sprinkler pipes were buried. Atop that layer came 40 to 50 miles of one-inch plastic hose to circulate water heated to 170 degrees. The purpose of the hot water was to jump-start growth of the turf—"to start the photosynthesis stage," Bossard explained, and compensate for spring's shade and low levels of direct sunlight.

The next layer was 5,000 tons of sand, 14 inches deep, and finally 106,000 square feet of turf grown near Olympia and at Woodinville. The sod was put down in May.

But the most important part of the field may be the clay, 600 tons of it, dug near Issaquah and used for the base paths and fielding positions. "Gator gumbo," a special blend of Mississippi clay imported from Illinois, was put down on the pitcher's mound and batter's boxes. It's a substance like pottery clay that permits a player's spikes to penetrate easily but also provides a solid grip.

One little-known fact about the groundskeeper's craft is that the keeper grooms the field to the taste of each home-team infielder. Some want the dirt soft; others want it hard.

To help along SAFECO Field's state-of-the-art field, Bossard introduced what he called his Sub-Air system, never before used in a major-league park. Essentially, it's a 150-horsepower machine that blows oxygen into the roots of the turf via the drain system and also sucks out the carbon dioxide produced by the grass.

The retractable roof, drain tile, 14 inches of sand, and blower system under the turf at SAFECO Field might lead an observer to suppose that it rains in the Northwest. Well, it does occasion-ally, and in that event Bossard is

The partially closed roof looms over the grandstand seats. (May 1999)

prepared. The system can drain up to 130,000 gallons of water and have the field ready for play 45 minutes after a deluge.

The resident head grounds-keeper at SAFECO Field is a 30-year-old protégé of Bossard, Steve Peeler, a former baseball player from Morganton, North Carolina. Peeler, who looks like a weightlifter or a baseball player—broad-chested and sturdy—worked with Bossard, his mentor, as head groundskeeper at Busch Stadium before coming to Seattle in December 1998.

After playing in an instructional professional league at St. Petersburg, Peeler realized he would not make it to the big leagues. Wanting to stay in base-ball in some capacity, he studied turf science at Catawba Valley Technical College in Hickory, North Carolina. It was a natural choice; he had started working with his grandfather on a golf course when he was only 6.

Peeler was building minor-league fields for the Chicago White Sox when he met Bossard, who took him under his wing. "He taught me, among other things, that the infield is the most important part of the field; it's where 80 percent of the action takes place," Peeler said. He and Bossard converted Busch Stadium in St. Louis from artificial turf to natural grass. "The turf was grown in Florida," Peeler recalled, "then brought to us in refrigerated trucks, timed so each truckload would arrive just when we needed it. It took us two days to put it down." Later he helped build 10 fields at the spring-training site the Cardinals and Expos share at Jupiter, Florida.

Peeler keeps in touch with the National Weather Service via computer, giving him access to all the high-tech equipment and data with which rainstorms and other phenomena are predicted. He can get the roof opened or closed—once started, it takes 20 minutes—depending on what's coming. He works closely on weather predictions with the umpires, who are in charge once presented with the lineup cards immediately before the game.

When the Mariners are playing a night game at home, Peeler's typical day starts long before game time. He begins work between 8:30 and 9 A.M. by dragging and smoothing the infield, then putting down gumbo clay in the batter's boxes.

At about 11 A.M., Peeler applies the heaviest watering of the day. Although he has four to eight people working with him, and perhaps 18 by game time, he trusts only himself to do the watering, which is more art than science. He waters again at about 12:30 P.M., also nail-dragging the infield to help the moisture sink into the soil. He mows daily after the heavy watering and sometimes mows a second time.

Throughout the day, Peeler maintains moisture on the mound and batting boxes by covering them with mats. Depending on the humidity, he may water once more before 6 P.M. He stays on the infield during batting practice,

dodging line drives, as he prepares each individual fielding position. He also fertilizes every week, alternating granular and spray fertilizer.

The other groundskeepers specialize; one mows, while another maintains the pitcher's mound. The cut grass is collected and disposed of as yard waste, although occasionally it's left on the field to help hold moisture.

The groundskeeper works closely with the team manager. After they have worked together for a time and understand each other's routines, they will not necessarily consult before every game. But make no mistake: the length of the grass is dictated by the manager. "If he wants a fast field, we will cut closer," Peeler said.

Overlooking the grounds is, the Mariners feel, the most compre-

hensive scoreboard system in all of baseball. It comprises 11 scoreboards and displays made by Daktronics of Brookings, South Dakota. The main scoreboard, in center field, is 56 feet high and 190 feet wide. It offers a huge state-of-the-art video screen capable of carrying high-definition TV signals when they become available. A companion matrix board displays graphics and

animation. In left field is an out-of-town scoreboard, 12 feet by 101 feet, showing innings, scores, and pitchers for games in progress in both leagues, plus a reader panel to highlight news and notes from other clubs.

Two play-by-play displays, 4 feet by 28 feet, the first of their kind in a major-league park, are positioned along the first- and third-base lines. They provide a

Much like a carpet layer, Larry A. Capps cuts the edge of the turf after it has been laid in place. By the end of the first week, head groundskeeper Steve Peeler was pleased to see the roots were growing. (May 1999)

Jeff Van Lierop watches as the turf is cut and rolled, while Merv Ward drives the tractor. Five hundred square feet of grass make up each two-ton roll. Over three nights, six trucks transported 270 rolls of the Kentucky bluegrass and perennial ryegrass blend from the Lacey turf farm to the ballpark. (May 1999)

running summary of plays. Four auxiliary displays, also along the first- and third-base lines, provide player at-bat information, pitch speed and type, and out-of-town game information. Three community-relations boards in right field display information about two service programs sponsored by the Mariners: "K's for Kids" and "Home Runs That Help." Finally, a hand-operated scoreboard in left field displays the line score of the game in progress.

Another nice touch in the grandstands is that most of the seats (44,000) are self-rising and have cup holders. Because the rows are only about half as long as those in the Kingdome, fans are never more than eight seats from an aisle. The concourses, too, are wider than at the Kingdome: up to 40 feet.

In December 1988, the Mariners opened the sale of tickets for the 42 games to be played during the 1999 season at SAFE-CO Field. The first day of public sale was typical raw Northwest weather: temperature in the low 40s, chilling rain whipping horizontally across the city. Undaunted, lines of couldn't-wait fans formed at ticket booths at the Kingdome. The lure of baseball played out-

doors was obvious from their comments.

Among the fans was Helge Spatz of Federal Way. He has followed the Mariners since they arrived in Seattle, attending about 10 games per year. Spatz was looking for tickets for Friday nights or Saturdays because he'd be able to sleep in the next morning after those games; he has to be at work "kind of early in the

Thom Ross mimics his art installation, **The Defining Moment.**

Gerard Tsutakawa directs workers installing his sculpture **The Mitt**.

*Peter Miner hooks a strap on
one of Ries Niemi's stainless
steel cutouts. (June 1999)*

A worker guides a stainless steel cutout into place. (June 1999)

*Brick pavers inscribed with fans' names are
placed in the Royal Brougham Fan Walk
in the Bullpen Market. (June 1999)*

morning" on weekdays. With him was his son Jacob, 11, who often accompanies his father to Mariners games.

Dan Rios of Kent, who moved to Seattle from Los Angeles 14 years ago and has followed the Mariners ever since, was also in line, buying tickets in the view section for the Yankees series and in the outfield for other games.

Bill Ferris of Seattle waited in his wheelchair, confident that there would be easy access to the new ballpark for people with disabilities. (His trust was well placed: more than 1,000 seats have been set aside for people with physical limitations.) Ferris was looking for tickets for July 16, the second game at SAFECO Field, because that is his wedding anniversary and his wife is "a bigger fan than I am."

Gerry Amarol, who said he gets asked if he's related to Rich Amaral, the former Mariners infielder, was buying tickets for his wife's birthday, which would take place during the Yankees series. "That series will probably be sold out relatively soon. So that's why I'm here."

John Marshall of Tacoma was enthusiastic about the new ball-park. "What could be better than watching baseball outdoors in the middle of summer in Seattle? It's going to be great!" He acknowledged it might be cold in April or October, "but it will be worth it. It doesn't matter. You're out there watching the game; bring some blankets or jackets and you'll be fine…. You know, I go down to Cheney Stadium in Tacoma and watch the games, and it's just great to be outdoors and watch the ballgames. I liked going to the Kingdome sometimes, but there was just one element missing. And that was being outside and enjoying it, because baseball is an outdoor sport. That's the way we used to play it when we were kids."

Bruce Decker of Seattle coached a Little League team in 1998. He was in line with his son Sam, 8, who, explained his father, "is just starting to get into baseball." Decker was looking for seats "down as low as possible, as close to the grass as I can get." Asked their favorite players, Decker named Ken Griffey Jr. and Alex Rodriguez. Young Sam also named Griffey, but his father added, "He plays catcher, so another favorite is Dan Wilson."

One of the things fans (particularly young ones like Sam) enjoy doing at ballparks is eating. Even without a poll, it's not difficult to surmise fans' priorities when they go to SAFECO Field. First is a Mariners victory. Second is easy access to a variety of good and fairly priced food and drink. Easy access to clean bathrooms might be third.

Fans, particularly female ones, will remember that the Kingdome's toilet facilities were inadequate. With a baseball seating capacity of almost 58,000, the Kingdome offered 189 toilets for women and 32 for men, as well as 225 urinals. SAFECO Field, in contrast, with a seating capacity of 47,000, has 259 toilets for women and 50 for men, as well as 225 urinals.

Regarding the second priority,

A couple enjoys the evening from Tsutakawa's **The Mitt**.

the Mariners' approach to food resembles the concept of the ballpark itself: back to tradition. Historically, what have fans eaten at baseball games? Hot dogs. So in their planning the concession-aires looked for the best hot dog they could find, placed on the best bun. Lots of everything else is being served, of course, from sushi to steak. But first and fundamentally, the Mariners want to offer the best hot dogs in town.

Keith Reardon of Volume Services America, the Mariners' new food supplier, expects to sell up to 1.5 million hot dogs each season. One-third of the crowd, or about 15,000 people, will eat full dinners at each game. They will have a wide variety of choices: full-service restaurants, four open-pit grills, a sports-bar restaurant, a pub, a food court, broilers, woks, raw bars for sushi and oysters, and outlets offering pizza and beer. "If you have good food at a fair price, people will want to eat there," declared Reardon.

With 47,000 fans wanting food—now!—fast service is essential. As a ballpark specialty, Volume Services America wanted to grill meat—hot dogs, hamburgers, steak—and place it on specially baked open-faced buns, in part to avoid wrapping. The big question was how to keep up with demand. The concessionaire decided on electric grills, which because of their power demands wouldn't have been feasible had the concept not been incorporated into the early planning of the park. Fortunately, it was worked into the design, providing SAFECO Field with a method of

food preparation unique among major-league parks.

Feeding thousands of fans who seem to get hungry simultaneously required careful long-term planning. A chart of the food facilities on the Main Concourse alone—listing restaurants, portable carts, espresso stands, and outlets offering hamburgers, pub beverages, hot roasted peanuts, fresh-squeezed lemonade, ice cream, and cookies, along with cooking and storage areas—is more complex than the casual eye can take in. One of SAFECO Field's virtues is that, because of the open concourses, fans can see the field and follow the game while at any of the food outlets.

Brad Schrock, the chief designer of Denver's Coors Field, was hired to advise the Mariners on luxury boxes, restaurants, retail spaces, and other areas within SAFECO Field controlled by the Mariners.

Team facilities at SAFECO Field are far superior to those in the Kingdome, Schrock declared. The Mariners' dugout and clubhouse are on the first-base side under the grandstand. One area of the clubhouse is devoted entirely to training, with a weight and exercise room, doctor's examination office, trainer's office, conditioning coach's office, and ample storage space for training. The other side of the clubhouse is primarily devoted to the home-team locker room, manager's office with its own shower and locker space, coaches' meeting room and locker room, team meeting room, player lounge with food tables, large shower and toilet facilities, and laundry facility.

"The wonderful thing about the complex," Schrock explained, "is that players have easy access to batting and pitching areas. So if they want to leave for half an inning to take batting practice, warm up a little bit, they're only 20 paces away from batting and pitching tunnels, side by side."

There's also a video training room with editing equipment, where tapes of previous games are stored. A window from that room looks into two complete batting and pitching tunnels, so practice there can be taped and later studied. The visitors' complex is nice but less elaborate, according to Schrock, with only one batting-pitching tunnel and scaled-down versions of the other components.

Another part of Schrock's purview was SAFECO Field's luxury suites. At other parks the suites are not congruent with the general ambience, looking more like corporate offices than comfortable spaces for relaxation and fun. Schrock's design avoided the corporate feel. "This is a Seattle and Pacific Northwest ballpark," he emphasized, "and ought to represent materials found in the Northwest, to give the feel of Pioneer Square's lofts, to go with NBBJ's overall design…. We wanted a comfortable, living-room feeling." To provide a loft-like atmosphere, ceilings are high—11 feet 6 inches—and are open visually to the structural steel above, bringing into the suites the rugged appearance of the rest of the grandstands.

On the theory that at most house parties, guests gather in the

Seats get a final washing. (June 1999)

Bleachers are inspected. (June 1999)

The ballpark's roof is retracted, creating a striking addition to the Seattle skyline. (June 1999)

The Home Plate Entrance is ready. (June 1999)

The last railings are installed. (July 1999)

The Mariners' red cedar dugout is cleaned. (June 1999)

SAFECO Field is silhouetted against the evening sky. (July 4, 1999)

Fans stream into the ballpark for the dedication ceremony. (July 5, 1999)

Former Seattle Rainiers outfielder K Chorlton shows his grandson Stone, 7 months, around the field after the dedication ceremony. (July 5, 1999)

Fireworks explode over the roof during Fourth of July celebrations.

Bruce Davis plays the trombone during the second public open house. (July 10, 1999)

Officials celebrate after cutting the ribbon during the dedication ceremony. (July 5, 1999)

kitchen, Schrock put big harvest tables in the center of the suites. The suites are heated and air-conditioned, and each has 16 armchairs. Cabinets are Douglas fir. Oriental rugs add warmth. Dinner can be ordered from special menus, served by special stewards.

The club seating level is just below the suites. The two areas are connected by a two-story space used for two club lounges, "with a big bar, lots of seats, and views to the outside," Schrock said. "On the first-base side, extensive glass allows views through the roof's track structure

all the way south, and you can see Mount Rainier. It's dramatic."

A continuous concourse along the club level, which holds 4,400 seats, is lined with glass. "If those in club seats want to get something to eat or drink, they pass through a set of doors; but because it's glass, they can stand there, eat or drink, and not lose sight of the game," Schrock noted. Servers also take orders at the seats, as at restaurants.

"On the club level we left exposed most of the structural steel that gets covered in most ballparks," Schrock said. "The structural steel is exposed. So the same green paint on exterior

structural steel penetrates inside and preserves the integrity of the park."

The Center Field Gate at the park opens three hours prior to each game, giving fans ample time to engage in interactive activities such as pitching and hitting in batting cages, playing Nintendo games, trading baseball cards, watching batting practice, and soaking up sun. "This is an exciting space," Schrock declared. "It opens to Royal Brougham Way, and the playing field is only slightly below street level. So there is visibility to the street, but also directly onto the playing field, over the bullpen in left field. The market space not only has game components, but pitching and batting cages as well as an interesting combination of food stands."

It takes 1,200 people to staff the food outlets. Long before the park opened, Volume Services America sent several thousand letters to various nonprofit organizations, giving them the opportunity to raise funds by providing servers. When a nonprofit organization contracts to provide at least 10 people per game for the season, they get 9 percent of sales. "It's better than a car wash, better than a bake sale," noted Reardon.

Artwork: A Big Mitt and Hutch's Windup

When fans aren't watching the game or eating, they may be admiring the baseball-oriented artwork displayed prominently throughout the park. The PFD allocated one-half of 1 percent of

the hard costs of the park, or $1.31 million, to artwork. The many strikingly original artworks are integrated into the structure of the ballpark.

William Gerberding, former president of the University of Washington, was chairman of the PFD's art selection committee. Janet Pelz, public affairs director for the PFD committee, called it "a dynamic, experienced group." The task it undertook was considerable. With the help of Irene Mahler, who assists individuals and corporations in acquiring art and who served as a consultant to the committee, notices were sent to 3,500 artists in Washington, Oregon, and British Columbia, asking for proposals. The 98 responses were culled to 16 artists, who were invited to make half-hour presentations.

From that number, nine were asked to develop proposals within six weeks. Sculptor Gerard Tsutakawa submitted an exact miniature of the nine-foot-tall mitt that today sits outside the park at First Avenue and Royal Brougham Way. Other presentations were more abstract but indicated the direction the artists would take. The committee eventually chose to commission eight of the works.

Ross Palmer Beecher of Seattle created the two large "quilts" mounted behind tempered glass in niches on facing walls at the Main Concourse level. One shows the logos of the current major-league teams; the other depicts baseball in the Pacific Northwest, from early to recent days. The artist incorporated license plates, old soda cans, and other metal

into her creations.

Tina Hoggatt of Issaquah, Washington, designed nine panels of porcelain enamel on steel that portray the nine fielding positions of baseball. They are mounted on columns on the outer side of the Upper Concourse in the north-west corner. Each measures three feet by five feet.

Helen Lessick of Seattle created five series of baseball trading cards, given away at games, that fans—notorious souvenir hunters—are already collecting. The cards feature baseball esoterica such as the sport's history, tradition, and rules.

Ries Niemi of Bow, Washington, contributed the stainless steel cutouts of pitchers and catchers mounted on park fences. His signature piece, above the northwest entry, shows nine fielders and a batter dressed and equipped as they would have been during various eras of the game.

Thom Ross of Seattle designed figures on painted stainless steel capturing various Mariners players at the instant Ken Griffey Jr. scored the run that beat the Yankees in the 1995 playoffs. The ecstatic scene is mounted at the top of the northwest entry stairs on the Main Concourse level.

Linda Beaumont, Stuart Keeler, and Michael Machnic of Seattle, known collectively as the Stable, created the 1,000 translucent bats that hang as a chandelier over the Rotunda behind home plate, as well as the geometric steel patterns on the gates, which were also designed by the artists. At the top of the grand staircase, which is stained in colors suggesting a churning sea, is a terrazzo compass rose 27 feet in diameter, a reference both to navigation and to the Mariners' logo. The rose features the signatures of all of the Mariners who were on the roster for the Inaugural Game on July 15, 1999.

Gerard Tsutakawa sculpted The Mitt, 9 feet tall and 12 feet wide, that stands just outside the northwest entrance.

Gu Ziong of Canada created the mural of porcelain enamel on steel in the northeast corner of the Main Concourse. It depicts a great variety of baseball-related items—from fans to 40 of baseball's greatest players to objects that might be seen at games, such as hot dogs or popcorn boxes.

Using a separate process, the art selection committee chose Donald Fels of Fall City, Washington, to provide metal relief sculptures for the parking garage. These show a hand on a baseball, each displaying the grip for one of six pitches: fastball, split-finger, curve, knuckler, slider, and change-up—an extensive repertoire for any pitcher. Fels also carved onto the columns of the garage a variety of baseball idioms, such as "out of left field" and "right off the bat."

Another special touch pays tribute to an icon of Seattle's baseball past. Attached to the seat at the end of each row is a wrought-iron relief cast of Fred Hutchinson, the young player from Seattle who enjoyed an illustrious career as a pitcher and manager in the major leagues. At the bottom of the design are Mount Rainier and a baseball

diamond. At the right end of each row the cast is reversed, showing Hutch pitching with his left hand. This is a bit of artistic license: Hutch was right-handed, not ambidextrous, but the reversal ensures that the figure of Hutch is always pitching toward the field.

One ballpark feature that signaled fan support was the sale of signed paving bricks, each engraved with a name, wish, or message. Ten thousand bricks were originally offered for sale at $75 each; after they sold out, the PFD offered an additional 2,500. The bricks are set in the Royal Brougham Fan Walk behind the left-field fence, grouped in discrete pods of 200 to 500 each. Proceeds from the bricks, each measuring 4½ by 9 inches, were in the $700,000 range and will help fund exhibits and fan activities at the ballpark's Northwest Baseball Museum.

Fans used the bricks to convey a variety of messages. Doug Rice wished "Andrew J. Gibb / Happy 10th B-day" and "Levi J. Rice / Happy 9th B-day." Alan Erfle honored "Jake & Tina Nist / Hitched 10/10/98." Other fans sent greetings to their favorite players: "April J. Weisman / A Dan Wilson Fan"; "Ted Hostikka / #1 Buhner Fan"; "Hit It Here Jr! / Ross & Laura." Others simply wished the Mariners well: "John, June & Rip / Say 'Go Mariners'"; "Russ and Anne Foss / World Series Here"; "Marinate 'Em / Pru Balatero." Two high school classes seized the opportunity to immortalize themselves: "Chelan and Greg / JFK Class of 1999" and "Thanks! Ms. Knodle / SWS

Class of 2000."

Barbara Smith and her two sisters purchased a brick in memory of their father, Clarence D. Smith. "Our father was a minor-league umpire who died about 25 years ago," she explained. "He was devoted to the game. He had three daughters but no sons, and we kids related to our father through baseball. When the paving-brick opportunity came up, we decided to buy a brick in his memory.

"We all have sons, and we have passed on our love of baseball to them. It's a big thing in our lives, part of our history, of our relationship with our children. I became a Mariners fan for the first season, and most years I have a season ticket. I'm the lone woman who stands to cheer the umpires when they are introduced." Family loyalty and love, solidarity, heritage, baseball as family fun—all encapsulated in a paving brick: "C. D. 'Smitty'/ World's Best Ump."

. . . .

Paul Nelson enjoys the view, as well as dessert, from the picnic area of the Rotunda. (July 8, 1999)

Sydney and Tom Hodge try out their season seats during the Hot Dog Gala. (July 8, 1999)

SAFECO Field waits silently for the Inaugural Game. (July 4, 1999)

"Fantastic" is how Chuck Szurszewski describes the ballpark. He, his wife,
Christina Meserve, and her sister Marlene Haslam attended the Hot Dog Gala, a benefit
for United Way of King County and the Fred Hutchinson Cancer Research Center. (July 8, 1999)

NATALIE FOBES

An Opening to Remember

Inaugural Day at SAFECO Field has arrived at last. The excitement is palpable.

The weather this day—it is July 15, 1999—hints of afternoon showers. By midafternoon a high overcast filters the sun. A woman wearing a heavy jacket trudges across the Kingdome parking lot to the adjacent ballpark. She remarks, "It's too hot for this thing." But she already knows an important fact about SAFECO Field: it is an open-air park, and some evenings will be nippy. Warm clothes are prudent.

Five hours before the game is to begin, crowds mill around the corner of First Avenue and Royal

92

FRED HOUSEL

Bathed in golden evening light, SAFECO Field is a diamond in the Emerald City. (July 15, 1999)

Fans line up to enter the Left Field Entrance hours before game time. For Joe Cox, waiting outside the Home Plate Entrance for 26 hours was a small price to pay for being the first fan through the gates. (July 15, 1999)

Excited fans arrive three hours before game time. (July 15, 1999)

The compass rose on the Main Concourse fills with fans exploring the ballpark.

Brougham Way outside the park. "Need 1 ticket," a sign implores. "High on Natural Grass," reads another. Street vendors of popcorn and cotton candy and programs hustle their wares. Royal Brougham, for whom the street is named—"Your Old Neighbor," as he called himself—might have written a corny "pome" (his spelling) about the lively scene for his column in the *Seattle Post-Intelligencer*, where years ago he was sports editor.

Inside, the San Diego Padres are taking batting practice. Sprinkled in the stands are 150 sailors from the USS *Carl Vinson*, an aircraft carrier stationed in Bremerton. Their white uniforms contrast smartly with the deep green seats. One sailor, Tom O'Connor of Danville, California, is a fan of the Oakland Athletics. But his companion, Kyle Wenck of Cherokee, Iowa, roots for the Mariners. They and their shipmates have volunteered to shoot the confetti guns that will be used later in the afternoon.

Up in the press box, seats have been assigned to a small battalion of writers. The opening of a new major-league ballpark is not as unusual as it was 15 years ago. But in the baseball world, the opening of SAFECO Field is still important. The writers represent such diverse publications and news organizations as *Baseball America*, AP, Reuters, the *Philadelphia Daily News*, the *Denver Post*, the *Milwaukee Journal*, and the *Detroit Free Press*. Writers from abroad are here too: Japan Pacific Publications, Tokyo FM, Sankei, Tokyo Chunichi. Also on hand are the commissioner of baseball, Bud Selig, and the president of the American League, Dr. Gene Budig.

Under the grandstands the umpires are rubbing up a special commemorative baseball. It is an official American League ball stamped with the SAFECO Field logo and the words "Inaugural Game, July 15, 1999." A special Inaugural Game logo has also been stitched onto the left side of the Mariners' caps.

The scene backstage is hectic. During the previous few days, three open houses, each of which drew 30,000 people or more, helped prepare personnel for the Inaugural Game. Now service personnel are getting final instructions. Program vendors, wearing shirts with Eddie Bauer logos on the back and left sleeve, cluster around their leader for

Jay Buhner jokes with Ken Griffey Jr. before the game.

Starting pitcher Jamie Moyer finds some quiet time in the Mariners' clubhouse.

Television personalities broadcast live from the Main Concourse.

NATALIE FOBES

BEN VANHOUTEN

Fireworks explode as maestro Gerard Schwarz conducts the Seattle Symphony during the pregame festivities.

NATALIE FOBES

With hands over their hearts, the Seattle Mariners and San Diego Padres line the base paths for the singing of the national anthem.

instructions. They are reminded that a half-hour lunch break is mandatory, but it isn't clear when they should take it. A pizza server is asked, "Are you going to be ready?" She replies confidently, "By four o'clock we certainly will be." Attendants at the Frozen

Rope Ice Cream booth are less certain. Only minutes before the gates are to open, they have no ice cream scoops. (The scoops arrive a few minutes later.)

Out in the Mariners' bullpen, the pitching coach, Stan Williams, is giving instruction to a young

pitcher whose warm-up jacket covers positive identification but who looks like Gil Meche.

Just outside the Home Plate Entrance at First Avenue and Atlantic Street, the Mariner Moose and announcer Rick Rizzs are entertaining hundreds of fans.

At 4 P.M., Rizzs leads the fans in a countdown: "Four, three, two, one, go!" The gates swing open. Into the ballpark and up the stairs, ignoring the escalators in the Rotunda, race a cascade of yelling, cheering, arm-waving fans. They have read about it,

Coach Stan Williams photographs friends and family.

KURT SMITH

Five-year-old Joey Hutchinson eyes the crowd before running the bases in honor of his grandfather, the late Fred Hutchinson.

NATALIE FOBES

David Segui signs autographs.

BEN VANHOUTEN

NATALIE FOBES

Alex Rodriguez smiles during the inaugural festivities.

NATALIE FOBES

His eyes alight, Anthony Pinza, 3, soaks up the atmosphere with his father, Paul.

heard about it, seen it on TV. Now they are in SAFECO Field!

At the smaller Left Field Entrance, entering fans wear broad smiles, happily greeting strangers. Some stop at the top of the stairs to listen to the Uptown Lowdown Jazz Band, a longtime Seattle institution, playing spirited Dixieland music. As fans enter the ballpark, the aroma of food drifts across the concourses, evoking the distinctive flavors of hot dogs, barbecue, and fish and chips.

Slowly the grandstands fill.

Out on the right-field grass—yes, grass!—Ken Griffey Jr., Jay Buhner, Edgar Martinez, and Alex Rodriguez are sprawled together, their Mariners teammates nearby, stretching their muscles. Griffey is doing more talking and laughing than stretching, perhaps because

he alone, of all the players, is clutching a bat.

Out behind the grandstand in right center field, Dylan Barnett from Little Kansas, Oklahoma, a 6-year-old blond with an infectious grin, is drying his wet feet. He has just toured the Children's

Dave Niehaus is choked with emotion as he learns he has been chosen to throw the first pitch.

The generations: Baseball legends and Little League players take positions on the field prior to the game.

NATALIE FOBES

BEN VANHOUTEN

BEN VANHOUTEN

BEN VANHOUTEN

Jamie Moyer winds up for the first pitch: **Steee-rike!**

It's back to work for Dave Niehaus as the game begins.

Jamie Moyer pitches.
Jay Buhner hits. Russ Davis fields.
It's baseball in SAFECO Field!

Playfield, completed only hours earlier, and somewhere stepped in a puddle. His father, Jeff Barnett of Seattle, seems unperturbed.

From a spot nearby, Seattle television and radio stations are broadcasting live throughout the day. In addition to features about SAFECO Field, KIRO-TV and KING-TV are broadcasting their regular newscasts from the ball-park. (The TV ratings for the Inaugural Game were the highest ever for a Mariners regular-season game.)

The formal ceremonies begin promptly at 6:15. Gerard Schwarz, wearing Mariners jersey number 1, leads the Seattle Symphony. The roof, closed an hour earlier, opens to the evening sky as the symphony plays the opening bars of Richard Strauss's *Also Sprach Zarathustra*, made familiar in recent years by the movie *2001: A Space Odyssey.*

Appropriately, it is Neil Skogland, the president of Ederer, the company that built the roof-opening mechanism, who presses the button that retracts the roof. Skogland had felt certain that honor would go to a club

Fans go wild as the Mariners come up to bat.

NATALIE FOBES

Not willing to miss one moment of the action, fans line the landings during the sold-out Inaugural Game.

executive or a public official. But he was chosen instead, perhaps because the Mariners wanted to be positive there would be no miscue.

As the roof opens, the crowd roars in appreciation. The weather for the Inaugural Game does not require a lid, but no doubt the roof's existence is giving comfort to more distant fans, who can be certain that a game will be played regardless of the possibility of showers. (To get ahead of our story: the roof was closed immediately after the first game. Good thing, too: heavy rain fell and thunderstorms rumbled overnight, and showers continued through the next day. The second and third games were played with the roof closed.)

Swiftly the program proceeds: a warm ovation for announcer Dave Niehaus, resplendent in black tie and tuxedo, who reads from W. P. Kinsella's *Shoeless Joe*, the basis of the movie *Field of Dreams*. Then it's the symphony's turn again, members donning Mariners caps and playing the *1812 Overture*, a cloud of smoke wafting across the field from the fireworks that have been substituted for the traditional cannons. A huge banner honoring Fred Hutchinson, the late major-league star from Seattle, is unfolded over the infield. Then Hutch's 5-year-old grandson runs the bases, ending at home plate in the arms of Griffey and Buhner.

NATALIE FOBES

Fans in the upper grandstand enjoy both the game and the spectacular sunset.

The mood of the ballpark changes as day gives way to evening.

The Padres players are introduced and greeted with congenial silence, followed by a loud standing ovation at the introduction of the Mariners. Deborah Voigt and Gary Lakes of the Seattle Opera sing the national anthem, accompanied by the symphony, and at last the field is cleared.

Not until it is announced on the public address system does Dave Niehaus learn that he has been chosen to substitute for Senator Slade Gorton in throwing out the opening pitch. Niehaus wipes away tears as the crowd roars approval. Not that anyone seems to care, but Niehaus's throw sails far over the head of Tom Foley, the former Speaker of the U.S. House of Representatives

and current ambassador to Japan, who is acting as catcher. Joked Niehaus later: "If he had better hands, he would have caught it."

It is almost game time now, and the crowd is getting hyped. To lusty cheers, players of the past, present, and future take positions on the field. Representing the past are veteran players for Seattle teams—the Mariners, the Pilots, the Rainiers, the Indians, the Steelheads. Among the veterans are former Mariners Alvin Davis, Harold Reynolds, and Ruppert Jones—the drawn-out cries of "Roooop! Roooop!" sound to the uninitiated like boos—as well as Jeneane DesCombs Lesko (who played in the Women's Professional Baseball

League), Eddie O'Brien, Lou Almada, Sherwood Brewer, Artie Wilson, and Edo Vanni. Alongside them, representing future players, are Little Leaguers at every position on the field. Finally, to noisy acclaim, come the players of the present: the Mariners.

As the tension mounts, Mariners hurler Jamie Moyer throws his warm-up pitches. At 7:14 P.M. the scoreboards blink "Play Ball." With fans on their feet and cameras flashing, Moyer throws his first pitch: *Steee-rike!*

The pregame ceremony has been so meticulously timed that it takes several innings for the crowd to realize they are no longer watching foreordained

events. Baseball's spontaneity and uncertainties unsettle spectators at first, turn them quiet, until a bad-hop single by San Diego over third base scores the first run, and the fans remember that victories and losses cannot be programmed.

At the same time, everyone recognizes the serendipity in the blaring horn blasts of Burlington Northern and Amtrak trains as they cross Royal Brougham Way just outside the park. Rather than a lonely wail, the kind evoked in Johnny Mercer's lyrics for "Blues in the Night," these are the sharp, urban hoots of a hustling city, and they give early signs of being one of the park's signatures (as do the shrill whistles of fans that break out spontaneously at the next

BEN VANHOUTEN

Alex Rodriguez connects.

KURT SMITH

The Padres score the first run.

KURT SMITH

David Bell scores.

KURT SMITH

Disappointment in the ninth.

KURT SMITH

game, on Friday night).

At about 8:30 the setting sun bursts through clouds and bathes the retracted roof and the top of the right-field stands with shimmering light. Those looking for a lucky omen are rewarded when Edgar Martinez promptly lines a single to right field. Those who scoff at heavenly signs are immediately affirmed, however, when Jay Buhner bounces into a double play.

The nature of the ballpark changes dramatically when night falls. Until then, alluring outside vistas—Seattle's skyline, Puget Sound, Mount Rainier, and the Olympics—attract the eye. But when it gets dark there is only the ballpark, transformed into a cocoon that shuts out the rest of the world. For those inside the park at nightfall, SAFECO Field becomes the center of the universe.

In six sections of the left-field bleachers, the Mariners have distributed red T-shirts with a bull's-eye on the chest, inviting the players to "Hit It Here." One shirt wearer is Margie Boslough of Vancouver, Washington, who seems charmed by both the sun and the ballpark. "It's absolutely gorgeous, wonderful," she exclaims. Back on the Main Concourse is Rick Kaminski, better known as Rick the Peanut

Man. He was a fixture at the Kingdome for 22 years, known for his behind-the-back tosses of peanut bags. His presence at the new stadium gives fans a sense of continuity. Nearby, on the third-base side of the Main Concourse, Alter Levitin of Seattle expresses his pleasure with the park. "It's beautiful," he says. "You can stroll and see everything. It's so crisp. I'm amazed."

Behind first base, Karen Fortier

103

Young and old watch from stair landings in right field during the Inaugural Game.

of Seattle calls SAFECO Field "awesome." Then, reflecting years of watching baseball indoors, she half-jokingly complains of being distracted by the airplanes, the sunset, the light breeze. "It's hard to focus," she says.

Leaving the ballpark after the game, Ted and Diana Barr of Bellevue and their 16-year-old son, Turner, sum up their reactions. The family has held season tickets for 20 years, and the Barrs have traveled to the last three All-Star games. Although their usual seats are elsewhere, at the Inaugural Game they sat in the top level of left field. Their verdict: SAFECO Field is better than Jacobs in Cleveland and Coors in Denver. "All the seats are good," they agree.

Despite a valiant eighth-inning rally, the Mariners lose their Inaugural Game at SAFECO Field, 3-2. The crowd is slightly subdued at the loss but nevertheless jubilant about the field.

After the game, manager Lou Piniella meets with scores of reporters. "It's a shame we didn't win," he says. "Walks have been our bugaboo, a thorn in our side all year." Still, he says, it is a great ballpark.

Not all games at SAFECO Field will hold the magic of the Inaugural Game, of course. This was New Orleans during Mardi Gras, Paris or Fremont celebrating the summer solstice, Seafair intensified. But finally, six years after the passage of enabling legislation, three years after the choice of the site, two years after the start of construction, one year after the roof went up, finally, after all those years, Inaugural Day had arrived. What a day it was to remember!

And what's the verdict of the sellout crowd of 44,607 fans? Piniella has it right: SAFECO Field is a great ballpark.

Yes, a great ballpark. But is that important? Deep down, does it really matter? We have seen how Camden Yards brought pride to Baltimore, how Jacobs Field stimulated the rejuvenation of Cleveland, how Coors Field led to the revival of a neighborhood in Denver. But ballparks do more than that. Good ballparks turn crowds into a massively extended family. They are places where, as A. Bartlett Giamatti, the late baseball commissioner, put it, crowds are transformed into a united community, a large family sharing common pain or pleasure.

Yes, SAFECO Field is a small town where people can come to share the enjoyment of the moment. The carpenters and ironworkers, the officials and the thousands of loyal fans all across the Pacific Northwest responsible for SAFECO Field intuitively knew that. A standing ovation, please, for those who made the dream of SAFECO Field come true.

NATALIE FOBES

. . . .

Buhner at bat . . . a new era in Seattle.

BEN VANHOUTEN

BEN VANHOUTEN

And the games continue...

The first home run: Russ Davis makes history.

Good players, good friends.

NATALIE FOBES

You gotta love these fans!

SCOTT EKLUND

SCOTT EKLUND

SCOTT EKLUND

It's Grand Salami time for Raul Ibanez!

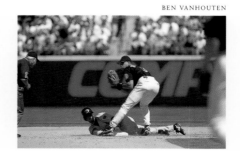

Griffey's first homer.

And the sun comes shining through.

"It's beautiful."

Alter Levitin, Seattle

111

John W. Ellis, Chairman and CEO of the Seattle Mariners, is a native of the Puget Sound region, and a lifelong baseball fan. He joined the Mariners as part of the founding ownership group in 1992, and is the owners' representative to Major League Baseball. He retired as Chairman and CEO of Puget Sound Power & Light (now Puget Sound Energy) in 1993. He lives in Bellevue.

Natalie Fobes is author and photographer of the award-winning books *Reaching Home: Pacific Salmon, Pacific People*; and *I Dream Alaska*. Her work is published in *Aubudon, Forbes, National Geographic, Smith-sonian, Time,* and other magazines.

A Pulitzer Prize finalist, Natalie is co-founder of Blue Earth Alliance, a nonprofit foundation dedicated to helping photographers pursue documentary projects. She lives in Seattle.

Frank Wetzel, a native of Bremerton, Washington, graduated from the University of Washington and worked for the Associated Press for 23 years in Salt Lake City, Denver, Baltimore, and Portland, Oregon. He then became editor of the *Journal-American* in Bellevue and later was ombudsman at *The Seattle Times.* He is author of *Victory Gardens and Barrage Balloons,* about the homefront during World War II. He lives in Seattle.

114